Panic Disorder and Agoraphobia

About the Author

Simon A. Rego, PsyD, ABPP, A-CBT, is chief of psychology and director of psychology training at Montefiore Medical Center and professor of psychiatry and behavioral sciences at Albert Einstein College of Medicine in the Bronx, New York. Dr. Rego is board certified in cognitive behavioral psychology by the American Board of Professional Psychology, certified in cognitive behavior therapy by the Canadian Association of Cognitive and Behavioural Therapies, and certified as a cognitive therapy trainer/consultant by the Academy of Cognitive and Behavioral Therapies. He is a fellow of the Association for Behavioral and Cognitive Therapies and the Academy of Cognitive and Behavioral Therapies, as well as a founding clinical fellow of the Anxiety and Depression Association of America. He is listed in *Who's Who in America* and *Who's Who in Medicine Academia*, and was the recipient of the 2002 Robert D. Weitz Award from the Graduate School of Applied and Professional Psychology at Rutgers University, the 2008 Virginia Staudt Sexton Award for Distinguished Early Career Psychologists by the New York State Psychological Association, the 2014 Peterson Prize from the Graduate School of Applied and Professional Psychology at Rutgers University, and the 2018 Jerilyn Ross Clinician Advocate Award from the Anxiety and Depression Association of America.

Advances in Psychotherapy – Evidence-Based Practice

Series Editor
Danny Wedding, PhD, MPH, Professor Emeritus, University of Missouri–Saint Louis, MO

Associate Editors
Jonathan S. Comer, PhD, Professor of Psychology and Psychiatry, Director of Mental Health Interventions and Technology (MINT) Program, Center for Children and Families, Florida International University, Miami, FL

J. Kim Penberthy, PhD, ABPP, Professor of Psychiatry & Neurobehavioral Sciences, University of Virginia, Charlottesville, VA

Kenneth E. Freedland, PhD, Professor of Psychiatry and Psychology, Washington University School of Medicine, St. Louis, MO

Linda C. Sobell, PhD, ABPP, Professor, Center for Psychological Studies, Nova Southeastern University, Ft. Lauderdale, FL

Larry Beutler, our esteemed Past Associate Editor, was the responsible scientific editor for this volume.

The basic objective of this series is to provide therapists with practical, evidence-based treatment guidance for the most common disorders seen in clinical practice – and to do so in a reader-friendly manner. Each book in the series is both a compact "how-to" reference on a particular disorder for use by professional clinicians in their daily work and an ideal educational resource for students as well as for practice-oriented continuing education.

The most important feature of the books is that they are practical and easy to use: All are structured similarly and all provide a compact and easy-to-follow guide to all aspects that are relevant in real-life practice. Tables, boxed clinical "pearls," marginal notes, and summary boxes assist orientation, while checklists provide tools for use in daily practice.

Continuing Education Credits

Psychologists and other healthcare providers may earn five continuing education credits for reading the books in the *Advances in Psychotherapy* series and taking a multiple-choice exam. This continuing education program is a partnership of Hogrefe Publishing and the National Register of Health Service Psychologists. Details are available at https://www.hogrefe.com/us/cenatreg

The National Register of Health Service Psychologists is approved by the American Psychological Association to sponsor continuing education for psychologists. The National Register maintains responsibility for this program and its content.

Advances in Psychotherapy – Evidence-Based Practice, Volume 55

Panic Disorder and Agoraphobia

Simon A. Rego
Montefiore Medical Center, The University Hospital for Albert Einstein
College of Medicine, Bronx, NY

Library of Congress of Congress Cataloging in Publication information for the print version of this book is available via the Library of Congress Marc Database under the Library of Congress Control Number 2024951773

Library and Archives Canada Cataloguing in Publication
Title: Panic disorder and agoraphobia / Simon A. Rego, Montefiore Medical Center, the University Hospital for Albert Einstein College of Medicine, Bronx, NY.
Names: Rego, Simon A., author.
Series: Advances in psychotherapy--evidence-based practice ; v. 55.
Description: Series statement: Advances in psychotherapy--evidence-based practice ; volume 55 | Includes bibliographical references.
Identifiers: Canadiana (print) 20250116839 | Canadiana (ebook) 20250116855 | ISBN 9780889374058 (softcover) | ISBN 9781616764050 (PDF) | ISBN 9781613344057 (EPUB)
Subjects: LCSH: Panic disorders. | LCSH: Panic disorders—Diagnosis. | LCSH: Panic disorders—Treatment. | LCSH: Agoraphobia. | LCSH: Agoraphobia—Diagnosis. | LCSH: Agoraphobia—Treatment. | LCSH: Cognitive therapy.
Classification: LCC RC535 .R34 2025 | DDC 616.85/223—dc23

© 2025 by Hogrefe Publishing. All rights, including for text and data mining (TDM), Artificial Intelligence (AI) training, and similar technologies, are reserved.

www.hogrefe.com

The authors and publisher have made every effort to ensure that the information contained in this text is in accord with the current state of scientific knowledge, recommendations, and practice at the time of publication. In spite of this diligence, errors cannot be completely excluded. Also, due to changing regulations and continuing research, information may become outdated at any point. The authors and publisher disclaim any responsibility for any consequences which may follow from the use of information presented in this book.

Registered trademarks are not noted specifically as such in this publication. The use of descriptive names, registered names, and trademarks does not imply, even in the absence of a specific statement, that such names are exempt from the relevant protective laws and regulations and therefore free for general use.

The cover image is an agency photo depicting models. Use of the photo on this publication does not imply any connection between the content of this publication and any person depicted in the cover image.
Cover image: © Jeff Bergen/peopleimages.com – Adobe Stock

PUBLISHING OFFICES

USA:	Hogrefe Publishing Corporation, 44 Merrimac St., Newburyport, MA 01950 Phone 978 255 3700; E-mail customersupport@hogrefe.com
EUROPE:	Hogrefe Publishing GmbH, Merkelstr. 3, 37085 Göttingen, Germany Phone +49 551 99950 0, Fax +49 551 99950 111; E-mail publishing@hogrefe.com

SALES & DISTRIBUTION

USA:	Hogrefe Publishing, Customer Services Department, 30 Amberwood Parkway, Ashland, OH 44805 Phone 800 228 3749, Fax 419 281 6883; E-mail customersupport@hogrefe.com
UK:	Hogrefe Ltd, Hogrefe House, Albion Place, Oxford, OX1 1QZ Phone +44 186 579 7920; E-mail customersupport@hogrefe.co.uk
EUROPE:	Hogrefe Publishing, Merkelstr. 3, 37085 Göttingen, Germany Phone +49 551 99950 0, Fax +49 551 99950 111; E-mail publishing@hogrefe.com

OTHER OFFICES

CANADA:	Hogrefe Publishing Corporation, 82 Laird Drive, East York, Ontario, M4G 3V1
SWITZERLAND:	Hogrefe Publishing, Länggass-Strasse 76, 3012 Bern

No part of this book may be reproduced, stored in a retrieval system or transmitted, in any form or by any means, electronic, mechanical, photocopying, microfilming, recording or otherwise, without written permission from the publisher.

Printed and bound in the USA

ISBN 978-0-88937-405-8 (print) · ISBN 978-1-61676-405-0 (PDF) · ISBN 978-1-61334-405-7 (EPUB)
https://doi.org/10.1027/00405-000

Dedication

I dedicate this book to the good people of the Bronx. The COVID-19 pandemic had a devastating impact on this largely underserved and underprivileged population – and yet they once again persisted in the face of adversity. I have never felt more pain for and, at the same time, more proud of a group, for never, ever giving up. I truly feel honored to have collaborated in the healing process of such an amazing and diverse community of people.

Acknowledgments

I am indebted to a large group of people, the first and foremost being the series editor, Danny Wedding; associate editor, Larry E. Beutler; and Robert Dimbleby, former publishing manager at Hogrefe Publishing, as much for their incredible patience and flexibility as for their invaluable guidance and suggestions along the way.

In many ways, the treatment plan described in this book is an amalgamation of the exceptional training and supervision provided to me, beginning 28 years ago when I entered Rutgers University's Graduate School of Applied and Professional Psychology, followed by my predoctoral internship year at the University of British Columbia Hospital, and finally during my first two postdoctoral years at the Center for Treatment and Study of Anxiety at the University of Pennsylvania in Philadelphia. Throughout this journey, I was very fortunate to be able to learn about the nature and treatment of panic disorder, obsessive-compulsive disorder, posttraumatic stress disorder, and a host of other disorders from some of the true luminaries in our field, including Edna Foa, Marty Franklin, the late great Arnold Lazarus, Deb Roth Ledley, Peter McLean, Lib Hembree, Jonathan Huppert, Bill Koch, Bob Leahy, Randy Paterson, Jack Rachman, Sheila Rauch, Dave Riggs, my mentor and friend Bill Sanderson, Maureen Whittal, and Terry Wilson, all of whom took a genuine interest in my professional development.

In addition, I owe a great deal to the many colleagues I have collaborated with during my 20+ years at Montefiore Medical Center and Albert Einstein College of Medicine, including my esteemed chair and dear friend, Jon Alpert, Greg Asnis, Bryan Freilich, Laurie Gallo, Alec Miller, Sandy Pimentel, Scott Wetzler, and Amanda Zayde. I also want to thank the psychology interns and fellows and psychiatry residents and fellows I have supervised over the years, who have forced me to stay on top of the literature by bringing such excellent questions into supervision and lectures.

Most of all, I want to thank my brilliant and beautiful wife, Dr. Adriana Rego, for her willingness to shoulder so much responsibility at home, so that I could focus on writing this volume. Without her constant help and support (and frequent encouragement), I would not have been able to complete this book.

Contents

Dedication		v
Acknowledgments		vii
1	**Description**	1
1.1	Terminology	1
1.2	Definition	1
1.3	Epidemiology	3
1.4	Course and Prognosis	4
1.5	Differential Diagnosis	6
1.5.1	Other Specified Anxiety Disorders or Unspecified Anxiety Disorder	6
1.5.2	Anxiety Disorder Due to Another Medical Condition	7
1.5.3	Substance- or Medication-Induced Anxiety Disorder	7
1.5.4	Other Mental Disorders With Associated Panic Attacks	7
1.5.5	Illness Anxiety Disorder	8
1.5.6	Specific Phobia, Situational Type	8
1.5.7	Separation Anxiety Disorder	9
1.5.8	Social Anxiety Disorder	9
1.5.9	Panic Disorder	9
1.5.10	Acute Stress Disorder and PTSD	9
1.5.11	Major Depressive Disorder	9
1.5.12	Other Medical Conditions	10
1.6	Comorbidities	10
1.7	Diagnostic Procedures and Documentation	11
1.7.1	Structured and Semi-Structured Diagnostic Interviews	11
1.7.2	Routine Outcome Monitoring	13
2	**Theories and Models**	15
2.1	The Cognitive Model	15
2.2	The Behavioral Model	18
3	**Diagnosis and Treatment Indications**	20
3.1	Diagnostic Assessment	20
3.2	Treatment Indications	21
3.2.1	Empirically Supported Treatments for Panic Disorder and Agoraphobia	21
3.3	Factors That Influence Treatment Decisions	26
3.3.1	Age	26
3.3.2	Gender	27
3.3.3	Race	28
3.3.4	Educational Level	28
3.3.5	Individual Preference	29
3.3.6	Social Support	29

3.3.7	Clinical Presentation and Comorbidity	30
3.3.8	Insight and Motivation	31
3.3.9	Patient's Treatment History	31
4	**Treatment**	**33**
4.1	The Diagnostic Assessment	34
4.2	Methods of Treatment	36
4.2.1	Presentation of the Principles of CBT and General CBT Model	36
4.2.2	Assessing Panic-Related Stimuli	39
4.2.3	Assessing Cognitive Features	40
4.2.4	Assessing Behavioral Features	41
4.2.5	Self-Monitoring	42
4.2.6	Psychoeducation	43
4.2.7	Using Cognitive Therapy Techniques	52
4.2.8	Planning for Interoceptive and In Vivo Exposure	54
4.2.9	The Power of Praise – and the Risks of Reassurance	66
4.2.10	Humor: Helpful or Hurtful?	66
4.2.11	Exposure for the Therapist	67
4.2.12	Booster Sessions	68
4.3	Mechanisms of Action	68
4.4	Efficacy and Prognosis	69
4.5	Variations and Combinations of Methods	70
4.5.1	Variants of CBT Treatment Procedures	70
4.5.2	CBT and Medications	70
4.6	Problems in Carrying out the Treatment	71
4.6.1	Organization of Suitable Treatment Settings or Preconditions	71
4.6.2	Negative Reactions to Psychological Interventions and the CBT Model	72
4.6.3	Resistance and Other Issues With Patient Motivation and Commitment	73
4.6.4	Therapist's Discomfort When Conducting Exposure Exercises	73
4.6.5	Therapist's Need to Provide Certainty	74
4.6.6	Problems in the Patient–Therapist Working Alliance	75
4.6.7	Cognitive Therapy Techniques and Somatic Skills That Become Safety Behaviors	75
4.6.8	Unbearable Anxiety Levels During Exposure	76
4.6.9	Absence of Anxiety During Exposure	76
4.7	Diversity Issues	77
5	**Case Vignette**	**79**
6	**Further Reading**	**84**
7	**References**	**85**
8	**Appendix: Tools and Resources**	**95**

1

Description

1.1 Terminology

Panic disorder first appeared as a specific diagnostic entity in the third edition of the *Diagnostic and Statistical Manual of Mental Disorders* (3rd ed.; *DSM-III*; American Psychiatric Association [APA], 1980), when the former *DSM-II* diagnosis of anxiety neurosis (APA, 1968) was divided into two separate entities: (1) panic disorder, which was characterized by spontaneous episodes of intense anxiety; and (2) generalized anxiety disorder, a residual category created for patients with chronic, sustained anxiety but without a reported history of panic attacks. Controversies surrounding the validity of the diagnostic criteria for panic disorder led to alterations of the definitions in both the *DSM III-R* (APA, 1987) and *DSM-IV* (APA, 1994). Also notable in the DSM-IV was the fact that panic attacks first became considered *transdiagnostic* (not exclusive to panic disorder). Instead, what became critical for making a diagnosis of panic disorder was the persistent fear of experiencing panic attacks, concern about the possible implications of a panic attack or the consequences of an attack, and/or the making of major behavioral changes due to a fear of the attacks. Finally, because a substantial number of patients reporting agoraphobia do not appear to experience panic symptoms, panic disorder and agoraphobia were unlinked in the *DSM-5* (APA, 2013). In so doing, the former DSM-IV diagnoses of panic disorder with agoraphobia, panic disorder without agoraphobia, and agoraphobia without a history of panic disorder were replaced in DSM-5 by two diagnoses in the *International Statistical Classification of Diseases and Related Health Problems* (10th ed.; *ICD-10*; World Health Organization, 2016): 300.01 (ICD-10 code F41.0) panic disorder and 300.22 (ICD-10 code F40.00) agoraphobia. As each of these diagnoses now has its own separate diagnostic criteria, the co-occurrence of panic disorder and agoraphobia should be coded by giving two diagnoses.

1.2 Definition

Panic disorder and agoraphobia are both classified as anxiety disorders in the DSM-5. The central feature of panic disorder is the experiencing of recurrent, unexpected panic attacks. A panic attack is defined as an abrupt surge of intense fear or discomfort (which can occur from either a calm or anxious state) that reaches a peak within minutes, and during which time four or more of a list of 13 physical (e.g., palpitations, pounding heart, or accelerated heart rate) and cognitive (e.g., fear of losing control or "going crazy") symptoms occur. At times, cultural concepts of distress (e.g., wind attacks in Cambodians in the US and Cambodia; *ataque de nervios* among Latin Americans, etc.) may also be observed, but these would not count toward the four required symptoms in the DSM-5. A panic attack that contains the abrupt surge of intense fear/discomfort that reaches a peak within minutes but with less than four of the 13 symptoms is a limited symptom attack.

Of note in the diagnostic features in the DSM-5 are the terms "recurrence" and "unexpected" as, taken together, this means that the person must have experienced more than one attack (i.e., a single attack would not warrant the diagnosis), and that at least one attack must have appeared to come on "out of the blue" (i.e., when the person was in a calm or relaxed state and with the person being unable to describe any obvious trigger at the time it happened). This may include panic attacks that occur as the person emerges from sleep (also known as nocturnal panic attacks – see Craske & Rowe, 1997). This distinction may in fact be helpful in differentiating panic disorder from other anxiety disorders, as it is typically the case with other anxiety disorders that the panic attacks have specific cues or triggers (e.g., patients with social anxiety disorder may get so anxious in social situations that they have a panic attack) and have never occurred in an unexpected manner. Interestingly, the frequency and severity of panic attacks can vary widely – both among patients diagnosed with panic disorder and throughout the course of the disorder in a patient diagnosed with panic disorder. According to the DSM-5, patients who have infrequent panic attacks resemble patients with more frequent panic attacks in terms of panic attack symptoms, demographic characteristics, comorbidity with other disorders, family history, and biological data (APA, 2013).

Finally, outside of the typical DSM-5 exclusionary criteria (e.g., the disturbance cannot be better accounted for by another mental disorder or by the physiological effects of a substance or medical condition), to be diagnosed with panic disorder, individuals must have at least 1 month of persistent concern/worry about experiencing further panic attacks or their physical consequences (e.g., having an undiagnosed, life-threatening illness), or social consequences (e.g., embarrassment and/or fear of being judged negatively if seen having a panic attack), and/or make significant maladaptive behavioral changes due a fear of the panic attacks (i.e., make substantial changes to their daily routines in order to avoid experiencing more panic attacks). If these maladaptive changes in behavior represent attempts to minimize or avoid panic attacks, or their consequences extend to two or more agoraphobic situations, then a separate diagnosis of agoraphobia would also be given.

The diagnostic criteria for agoraphobia, which was unlinked from panic disorder in the DSM-5, were derived from the DSM-IV descriptors for agoraphobia, with the main change in the DSM-5 being that the patient must endorse a marked fear of two (or more) of five common agoraphobia situations (i.e., public transportation, being in open spaces, being in enclosed places, standing in lines or being in crowds, being outside the home alone), as this is believed to be a robust means for distinguishing agoraphobia from specific phobias (APA, 2013). In addition, the criteria for agoraphobia were extended to be consistent with the criteria sets for other anxiety disorders (e.g., the fear, anxiety, or avoidance must be persistent for 6 months or more, must cause clinically significant distress or impairment, cannot be better explained by another mental disorder).

1.3 Epidemiology

Despite decades of research on the epidemiology of anxiety disorders, surprisingly little has been published on their *incidence*. In fact, in a systematic review of the literature published between 1980 and 2004 reporting findings of the prevalence and incidence of anxiety disorders in the general population, Somers et al. (2006) found that "An insufficient number (n = 5) of incidence studies were available for inclusion, signaling an important omission in the epidemiologic literature" (p. 100). They concluded that, "Further knowledge is required about the onset of anxiety disorders, including risk and protective factors, as well as social variables that may mediate the expression of these disorders and help explain the level of heterogeneity observed in the present study" (p. 111).

Fortunately, much more data exist on their *prevalence*. For example, according to the National Institute of Mental Health (NIMH), the *lifetime prevalence* estimate for panic disorder across the US adult population is 4.7% (Kessler, Berglund et al., 2005). According to the DSM-5, the 12-month prevalence estimate for panic disorder across the US and several European countries in the general population is about 2–3% in adults and adolescents. While children do experience panic *attacks*, panic *disorder* (and agoraphobia) are low-prevalence conditions in childhood (1% or lower), with slightly higher prevalence rates (2–3% for panic disorder and 3–4% for agoraphobia) found in adolescence (Beesdo et al., 2009). While the low rate of panic disorder in children could relate to difficulties in symptom reporting, this seems to be unlikely given that children are capable of reporting intense fear or panic in relation to separation and difficult objects or phobic situations (APA, 2013).

The prevalence rates of panic disorder show a gradual increase during adolescence, particularly in females (who ultimately end up diagnosed at twice the rate of males) and possibly following the onset of puberty, and peak during adulthood (APA, 2013). According to the NIMH, the average age of onset is 24 years old (Kessler, Chiu et al., 2005). The prevalence rates then decline in older individuals (e.g., the prevalence is 0.7% in adults over the age of 64 years), possibly reflecting a diminishing severity to subclinical levels due to what appears to be an age-related dampening of the autonomic nervous system response (APA, 2013). In addition, older adults tend to attribute their panic attacks to stressful situations (e.g., medical procedures or social settings) and may retrospectively endorse these as explanations for a panic attack. This is important to note, as it would preclude the diagnosis of panic disorder even if the attack might have actually been unexpected in the moment (APA, 2013). Thus, careful questioning of older adults is required to ensure that a diagnosis of panic disorder is not overlooked.

Finally, in the US, significantly lower rates of panic disorder are reported among Latinx, African Americans, Black Caribbeans, and Asian Americans compared with non-Latinx Whites, while Native Americans have significantly higher rates (APA, 2013). Outside of the US, however, lower estimates of rates ranging from 0.1% to 0.8% have been reported for Asian, African, and Latin American countries (APA, 2013).

According to the DSM-5, the 1-year prevalence of agoraphobia in the US is approximately 1.7% for adolescents and adults, and 0.4% for individuals older than 65 years. It may occur in childhood, but its incidence peaks in late adolescence and early adulthood. Prevalence rates do not appear to vary systematically across cultural/racial groups, but females are twice as likely as males to experience it.

> Females are more than twice as likely as males to experience agoraphobia

1.4 Course and Prognosis

While children can experience panic attacks, the overall prevalence of panic disorder is less than 0.4% before age 14 years. Similarly, onset after age 45 years is unusual, but can occur (APA, 2013). Instead, panic disorder typically starts in young adulthood, with the median age of onset in the US being approximately 24 years (Kessler, Chiu et al., 2005). To date, no differences in the clinical presentation between adolescents and adults have been found; however, adolescents may be less worried than young adults about additional panic attacks (APA, 2013).

Naturalistic longitudinal studies indicate that the course of untreated panic disorder can be chronic and disabling (Barlow, 2004). Factors associated with poor outcome include early onset of illness and phobic avoidance (Yonkers et al., 1998). According to the DSM-5, some patients may have episodic outbreaks with years of remission in between, while others may have continuous severe symptomatology. Only a minority of untreated individuals, however, experience full remission without subsequent relapse within a few years (APA, 2013). Relapse rates are higher among women than men (Yonkers et al., 1998). People with panic disorder are, compared with healthy controls, at a greater risk for a significant impairment in quality of life and in the social and economic environment (Lochner et al., 2003). Finally, as noted in the DSM-5, the course of panic disorder is typically complicated by a range of other comorbid disorders – particularly other anxiety disorders, depressive disorders, and substance use disorders (APA, 2013).

The mean age of onset for agoraphobia is 17 years, although the age of onset without preceding panic attacks or panic disorder is later (25–29 years). In two thirds of all cases of agoraphobia, the initial onset occurs before age 35 years. It appears that there is a substantial incidence risk at two ages: (1) late adolescence and early adulthood, and (2) after age 40 years. First onset in childhood is rare.

The course of agoraphobia is typically persistent and chronic (APA, 2013) and, if untreated, complete remission is rare (approximately 10%). As the severity of agoraphobia increases, the rates of full remission decrease, and the rates of relapse and chronicity increase. Finally, as noted in the DSM-5, and as is the case for panic disorder, a range of other comorbid disorders (see Section 1.5) – particularly other anxiety disorders, depressive disorders, substance use disorders, and personality disorders – may complicate the course of agoraphobia, and the long-term course and outcome of agoraphobia are associated with substantially elevated risk of secondary major depressive disorder, persistent depressive disorder (dysthymia), and substance use disorders.

Fortunately, the prognosis is very good if the panic disorder and/or agoraphobia is treated, and a number of interventions – including both psychological (e.g., cognitive behavioral therapy [CBT]) and pharmacological treatments – are available with a substantial evidence base supporting their efficacy and effectiveness. For example, in one longitudinal study of CBT, 87% of patients initially diagnosed with panic disorder were panic free at the end of treatment, with 96% remaining in remission at 2-year follow-up, 77% at 5-year follow-up, and 67% at 7-year follow-up (Fava et al., 1995). CBT has also been found to effective in associated depressive symptoms and in increasing quality of life (Mitte, 2005). In addition, the scheduling of periodic CBT "booster" sessions has been shown to reduce relapse rates (e.g., White et al., 2013).

First-line acute pharmacological treatments include different selective serotonin reuptake inhibitors (SSRIs), such as paroxetine, fluoxetine, citalopram, sertraline, and escitalopram, as well as the serotonin-norepinephrine reuptake inhibitor (SNRI) venlafaxine. Of the individual SSRIs, a recent systematic review and network meta-analysis of randomized controlled trials by Chawla et al. (2022) suggested that sertraline and escitalopram provided high remission with low risk of adverse events, though the authors cautioned that their findings were based on studies of moderate to very low certainty levels of evidence. While high-potency benzodiazepines (e.g., lorazepam, alprazolam, and clonazepam) have been found to be effective – alone or as adjunctive to SSRIs – in treating panic disorder with or without agoraphobia, their use presents several serious clinical issues, such as rebound anxiety, memory impairment, discontinuation syndrome, and a potential for abuse and dependence (Pull & Damsa, 2008). Expert consensus guidelines suggest that pharmacological treatments for panic disorder should be continued for at least 1 year from the point of treatment response, to help ensure symptom reduction and protection against relapse, as relapse rates following medication discontinuation are estimated to be between 55% and 70% (Ballenger et al., 1993), with discontinuation of benzodiazepines being associated with an even higher risk for relapse (Ballenger et al., 1993). As a result, the long-term management of panic disorder with or without agoraphobia using pharmacological treatments requires adequate dosing

Benzodiazepines can result in rebound anxiety, memory impairment, and discontinuation syndrome, and they can potentially result in abuse and dependence

and attainment of maximal functioning before medication discontinuation (Doyle & Pollack, 2004).

Interestingly, while combining pharmacological treatment with CBT has been found to be superior to pharmacological treatment or CBT alone, it appears to only be the case in the acute phase of treatment (Pull & Damsa, 2008). In the long-term treatment of panic disorder with or without agoraphobia, combining pharmacological treatment with CBT may be more effective than pharmacological treatment alone, but does not appear to be more effective than CBT alone (Pull & Damsa, 2008). An added benefit of combining pharmacological treatment with CBT, however, may be in managing relapse (Furukawa et al., 2007) for those on pharmacological treatments but wanting to discontinue them. In addition, some patients may benefit from remaining on maintenance pharmacotherapy along with booster CBT sessions in order to protect against relapse over the longer term.

1.5 Differential Diagnosis

The symptoms of panic disorder and agoraphobia often overlap with other disorders

In clinical practice, panic disorder and agoraphobia can, at times, be difficult to differentiate from a number of other disorders that share similar symptom patterns. Therefore, the aim of this section is to highlight some of the key differences between the symptoms of panic disorder and agoraphobia and those of several other disorders (including one another). The most common differential diagnoses for panic disorder include: (a) other specified or unspecified anxiety disorder, (b) anxiety disorder due to another medical condition, (c) substance/medication-induced anxiety disorder, (d) other mental disorders with panic attacks as an associated feature, and (e) illness anxiety disorder. Each of these will be described Sections 1.5.1 to 1.5.5.

1.5.1 Other Specified Anxiety Disorders or Unspecified Anxiety Disorder

As noted in Section 1.2, some individuals may only report experiencing limited symptom unexpected panic attacks. According to the DSM-5, in these cases, the diagnoses of other specified anxiety disorder (used in situations in which the clinician chooses to communicate the specific reason that the presentation does not meet the criteria for any specific anxiety disorder) or unspecified anxiety disorder (used in situations in which the clinician chooses not to specify the reason that the criteria are not met for a specific anxiety disorder, and includes presentations in which there is insufficient information to make a more specific diagnosis) should be considered.

1.5.2 Anxiety Disorder Due to Another Medical Condition

A common diagnostic criterion found throughout the DSM-5 is that the disturbance is not attributable to another medical condition. In the case of panic disorder, it is important to rule out any potential medical conditions that could be causing the panic attacks – be they unexpected or not. Examples of medical conditions that can cause panic attacks include hyperthyroidism, vestibular dysfunctions, hyperparathyroidism, seizure disorders, and cardiopulmonary conditions. In addition, features such as onset after 45 years of age or the presence of atypical symptoms during a panic attack, such as vertigo, loss of consciousness, loss of bladder or bowel control, slurred speech, or amnesia, suggest the possibility that another medical condition may be causing the panic attack symptoms. As such, it is always a good idea to ensure that a newly referred patient has recently undergone a thorough physical examination that includes a comprehensive metabolic panel.

> It is especially important to rule out other medical conditions with recent onset in older patients or when the presentation is atypical

1.5.3 Substance- or Medication-Induced Anxiety Disorder

Another common diagnostic criterion found throughout the DSM-5 is that the disturbance is not attributable to the physiological effects of a substance. This can include both drugs of abuse as well as medications. In this case, panic disorder would not be diagnosed if the panic attacks were assessed to be the direct physiological consequence of a substance. Examples of drugs of abuse include intoxication with central nervous system stimulants (e.g., cocaine, amphetamines, caffeine) or cannabis and/or withdrawal from central nervous system depressants (e.g., alcohol or barbiturates). Examples of medications include asthma medications (e.g., albuterol, salmeterol), blood pressure medications (e.g., methyldopa), and hormones (e.g., oral contraceptives).

A diagnosis of panic disorder should be considered if the panic attacks continue to occur long after the effects of the intoxication or withdrawal should have ended (APA, 2013). In addition, because individuals experiencing panic attacks may increase their use of substances (e.g., alcohol) in an effort to cope, it is important to take a detailed timeline in order to determine if the panic attacks *preceded* the substance use. If this is the case, then a diagnosis of panic disorder should be considered in addition to a diagnosis of a substance use disorder (APA, 2013).

> Some patients will attempt to treat their anxiety by self-medicating with alcohol or other substances

1.5.4 Other Mental Disorders With Associated Panic Attacks

The DSM-5 stipulates that the disturbance should not better be accounted for by the presence of another mental disorder. For example, if the panic attacks only occur in response to feared social situations, a diagnosis of social anxiety disorder should be considered. Similarly, if the panic attacks only occur in response to the re-experiencing symptoms of a traumatic event, a diagnosis of either acute stress disorder or posttraumatic stress disorder (PTSD) would instead be considered. Panic disorder should only be diagnosed if recurrent, unexpected full-symptom panic attacks have been experienced. If the individual begins to experience recurrent, unexpected panic attacks in addition to expected attacks, and then shows persistent concern or worry and/or makes behavioral changes because of the attacks, an additional diagnosis of panic disorder should be considered (APA, 2013).

1.5.5 Illness Anxiety Disorder

In panic disorder, the patient may be concerned that the panic attacks reflect the presence of a medical illness; however, although these patients report feeling anxious about their health, their anxiety is typically very acute and episodic. In illness anxiety disorder, the health anxiety and fears are more persistent and enduring. Much like is the case for patients with generalized anxiety disorder (GAD), who can experience panic attacks when worrying excessively about many everyday life events, and patients with illness anxiety disorder, who may become so concerned about their illness that they experience panic attacks.

Common differential diagnoses for agoraphobia include: (a) specific phobia, situational type, (b) separation anxiety disorder, (c) social anxiety disorder, (d) panic disorder, (e) acute stress disorder and PTSD, (f) major depressive disorder, and (g) other medical conditions. Each of these will be described in Sections 1.5.6 to 1.5.12.

1.5.6 Specific Phobia, Situational Type

Differentiating agoraphobia from the situational subtype of specific phobia can be challenging in some cases, because the conditions share several symptom characteristics and criteria. As such, the DSM-5 suggests only diagnosing the situational subtype of specific phobia if the fear, anxiety, or avoidance is limited to one agoraphobic situation, and diagnosing agoraphobia if the fear, anxiety, or avoidance extends to two or more agoraphobic situations. In addition, examining the beliefs associated with the fear, anxiety, or avoidance can differentiate agoraphobia and the situational subtype of specific phobia. That is, if the situation is feared for reasons other than panic-like symptoms or other incapacitating or embarrassing symptoms (e.g., fears of being directly harmed by the situation itself, such as fear of the plane crashing for individuals who fear flying), then a diagnosis of the situational subtype of specific phobia may be more appropriate (APA, 2013).

1.5.7 Separation Anxiety Disorder

Separation anxiety disorder can also be best differentiated from agoraphobia by examining the beliefs associated with the fear, anxiety, or avoidance. As the name suggests, in separation anxiety disorder the central theme of the fear-related beliefs is about being detached (i.e., separated or disconnected) from significant others and the home environment (i.e., parents or other attachment figures), whereas in agoraphobia the central theme of the fear-related beliefs is the symptoms of panic and/or other incapacitating or embarrassing symptoms the individual may experience in the feared situations.

1.5.8 Social Anxiety Disorder

As was the case with the situational subtype of specific phobia and separation anxiety disorder, agoraphobia can also be differentiated from social anxiety disorder based on both the situations that trigger the individual's fear, anxiety, or avoidance, as well as the beliefs associated with the fear, anxiety, or avoidance. In social anxiety disorder, the focus of the fear-related beliefs is on being negatively evaluated.

1.5.9 Panic Disorder

As was the case with the situational subtype of specific phobia, when criteria for panic disorder are met, agoraphobia should not be diagnosed if the avoidance behaviors associated with the panic attacks do not extend to avoidance of two or more agoraphobic situations.

1.5.10 Acute Stress Disorder and PTSD

Acute stress disorder and PTSD can be differentiated from agoraphobia by examining whether the fear, anxiety, or avoidance is related only to situations that remind the individual of a traumatic event. If the fear, anxiety, or avoidance is restricted to trauma reminders, and if the avoidance behavior does not extend to two or more agoraphobic situations, then a diagnosis of agoraphobia would not be warranted.

1.5.11 Major Depressive Disorder

In major depressive disorder, the patient may avoid leaving home due to low energy, anhedonia, a sense of apathy, and/or low self-esteem. As such, if the avoidance appears to be unrelated to fears of panic-like or other incapacitating or embarrassing symptoms, then agoraphobia should not be diagnosed.

1.5.12 Other Medical Conditions

Agoraphobia would not be diagnosed if the avoidance of situations is judged to be the result of a physiological consequence of a medical condition or age-related symptoms – as determined based on a history, laboratory findings, and a physical examination. Other medical conditions that may be relevant include neurodegenerative disorders with associated motor disturbances (e.g., Parkinson's disease, multiple sclerosis), as well as cardiovascular disorders. Patients with certain medical conditions may avoid situations because of realistic concerns about being incapacitated (e.g., fainting in a patient with transient ischemic attacks) or embarrassed (e.g., diarrhea in a patient with Crohn's disease). As such, the diagnosis of agoraphobia should be given only when the fear or avoidance is clearly in excess of that usually associated with these medical conditions (APA, 2013).

1.6 Comorbidities

> Comorbidities are extremely common with panic disorder

Panic disorder frequently occurs in clinical settings along with other pathology. In fact, one study found that 98% of panic disorder patients had at least one comorbid disorder (Tilli et al., 2012). For example, panic disorder is often diagnosed comorbidly with mood disorders, with reported lifetime rates of comorbidity between major depressive disorder and panic disorder varying widely, and estimates ranging from 10% to 65% in patients with panic disorder. In addition, patients with panic disorder appear to be at higher risk of suicide when compared to the general population, with one study finding that patients with panic disorder were approximately twice as likely as those without panic disorder to present at an inner-city primary care clinic with current suicidal ideation (Pilowsky et al., 2006). In addition, the prevalence of panic disorder is elevated in patients with other psychiatric disorders, particularly other anxiety disorders (and especially agoraphobia), and bipolar disorder (APA, 2013), as well as schizophrenia, obsessive-compulsive disorder, specific phobias, and social anxiety disorder (Buckley et al., 2009). Comorbidity with illness anxiety disorder is also common (APA, 2013). Furthermore, approximately 10–20% of patients with panic disorder abuse alcohol and other drugs, and about 10–40% of patients with alcohol use disorder have a panic-related anxiety disorder (Cox et al., 1990). According to the DSM-5, for some patients, this represents an attempt to treat their anxiety with alcohol or other drugs (including medications).

> Patients with panic disorder are at greater risk for sudden death
>
> There is a strong association between panic disorder and asthma

While panic disorder is also significantly comorbid with numerous general medical symptoms and conditions, according to the DSM-5 the *nature* of the association (e.g., cause and effect) between panic disorder and these conditions remains unclear. Notable general medical symptoms and conditions include cardiovascular disorders such as mitral valve prolapse, hypertension, cardiomyopathy, stroke (Chen et al., 2010), chronic obstructive pulmonary disease, irritable bowel syndrome, restless leg syndrome, and fatigue (Lee et al., 2008; Kaiya et al., 2008), dizziness, cardiac arrhythmias, hyperthyroidism (APA, 2013), and migraine headaches (12.7%), tension headaches (5.5%), and combined migraine and tension headaches (14.2%) (Beghi et al., 2007). Patients with panic disorder are also nearly twice as likely to develop coronary artery disease, and patients with both panic disorder and coronary artery disease can experience myocardial ischemia during their panic episodes (Fleet et al., 2005; Gomez-Caminero et al., 2005). As a result, panic disorder is also associated with a higher risk of sudden death (Sullivan et al., 2004). Finally, individuals with asthma have 4.5 times increase in the risk of developing panic disorder, and people with panic disorder are 6 times as likely as those without anxiety disorders to develop asthma (Hasler et al., 2005). While panic disorder often has an earlier age of onset than the comorbid disorder(s), the onset sometimes occurs after the comorbid disorder and thus may be seen as a severity marker of the comorbid illness. For example, in approximately one third of patients with both major depressive disorder and panic disorder, the depression precedes the onset of panic disorder, while in the remaining two thirds the depression occurs either coincident with or following the onset of panic disorder (APA, 2013).

As is the case for patients with panic disorder, the majority of patients with agoraphobia also have other comorbid mental health disorders (APA, 2013). The most frequent additional diagnoses are other anxiety disorders such as specific phobia(s), panic disorder, and social anxiety disorder; depressive disorders (e.g., major depressive disorder), PTSD, and alcohol use disorder. Whereas some anxiety disorders such as separation anxiety disorder, specific phobia(s), and panic disorder frequently precede onset of agoraphobia, depressive disorders (e.g., major depressive disorder) and substance use disorders typically occur secondary to agoraphobia (APA, 2013).

1.7 Diagnostic Procedures and Documentation

This section reviews evidence-based structured and semi-structured diagnostic interviews that can be used confirm the diagnoses of panic disorder and agoraphobia (in addition to identifying other common comorbid disorders and aiding in differential diagnosis), as well as evidence-based routine outcome monitoring self-report measures that can be used for assessing the severity of panic disorder and agoraphobia symptoms, as well as for documenting changes occurring in these symptoms over the course of treatment.

1.7.1 Structured and Semi-Structured Diagnostic Interviews

Currently, there are several evidence-based structured and semi-structured diagnostic interviews to choose from. The three most commonly used are: (1) the Structured Clinical Interview for DSM Diagnoses (SCID), (2) the

There are three well-established, evidence-based diagnostic interviews

Anxiety and Related Disorders Interview Schedule (ADIS-5; formerly known as the Anxiety Disorders Interview Schedule), and (3) the Mini International Neuropsychiatric Interview (MINI). Each of these instruments has strong psychometric properties (i.e., good reliability and validity). Each of these is described in more detail in the following sections.

The SCID

The SCID is a semi-structured interview for making sure that the major DSM clinical disorder diagnoses are systematically evaluated (note: there are also two separate SCID versions aimed at assessing personality disorders as presented in the DSM-5). Several different versions of the SCID are available, including a research version (First et al., 2015) and a clinician version (First et al., 2016). The average administration time of the SCID can vary greatly, depending on the extent and complexity of the patient's psychopathology and psychiatric history. As such, the range in administration time has been estimated from about 15 minutes (i.e., for a patient presenting with virtually no psychopathology or psychiatric history) to several hours (i.e., for a patient with extensive psychiatric comorbidity, a long psychiatric history, and with a tangential and/or circumstantial style of speech), with the average administration time of the full research version of the SCID estimated at 90 minutes. All versions of the SCID (along with training tapes, interview guides, and response booklets) are copyrighted and must be purchased through American Psychiatric Association Publishing (https://www.appi.org/scid5).

The ADIS-5

The ADIS is a structured interview designed in part to assess for current episodes of anxiety disorders, in part to permit the differential diagnosis among the anxiety disorders according to DSM criteria, and in part to provide sufficient information to permit a functional analysis of the anxiety disorders to be performed. In addition, the ADIS includes modules that assess for current mood, somatoform, and substance use disorders, due in part to their high comorbidity with the anxiety disorders and in part due to the fact that these disorders often present as symptomatically similar to the anxiety disorders. The ADIS also contains screening questions for psychotic and conversion symptoms and familial psychiatric history, as well as a more detailed section aimed at assisting in ascertaining the patient's medical and psychiatric treatment history.

As is the case with the SCID, the ADIS is also currently available in several different forms. These include an adult version (ADIS-5-Adult Version; Brown & Barlow, 2014a) and a lifetime version (ADIS-5L; Brown & Barlow, 2014b). The ADIS-5L contains all of the sections included in the regular ADIS-5, while also being designed to establish past (i.e., lifetime) diagnoses, as well as a diagnostic timeline to assist in the determination of the onset, remission, and temporal sequence of current and past disorders. The average administration time of the ADIS-5 is estimated at 90 minutes, but some studies have reported much longer times, depending on the population and the extent of the patient's psychopathology, psychiatric history, and style of speech. It is suggested that clinicians administering the ADIS be trained on how to conduct the interview, and a clinician's manual has been developed for both the ADIS-5 and the ADIS-5L. All versions are available from Oxford University Press.

The MINI

The MINI is a short, structured diagnostic interview that was developed in 1990 by psychiatrists and clinicians in the US and Europe for DSM-IV and ICD-10 psychiatric disorders (Sheehan et al., 1998). While the standard MINI does not provide the same level of detail as the SCID or ADIS, it is much briefer (estimated administration time of the standard MINI is approximately 15 minutes) and has been validated against the SCID, the Composite International Diagnostic Interview for ICD-10, and even against expert opinion in a large sample in four European countries (France, United Kingdom, Italy, and Spain). As such, it is considered by many researchers to be a fully validated and more time-efficient alternative to the SCID and ADIS (although in 2021 a briefer, more time-efficient version of the SCID, designed to be administered usually in 30 minutes or less, called the Quick Structured Clinical Interview for DSM-5 Disorders [QuickSCID-5] was released).

> Administration time for the MINI is much shorter than that for the SCID and ADIS

Like the SCID and ADIS, the MINI is currently available in several different forms (all of which are bundled into a "MINI Suite" by the publisher), including the standard MINI (which also is available in different languages), the MINI Plus (which is more comprehensive in disorders assessed), the MINI for ADHD Studies, the MINI for Schizophrenia and Psychotic Disorders Studies, the MINI Kid (available in numerous languages), the MINI Kid for Schizophrenia and Psychotic Disorders Studies, and a MINI screening tool. The MINI suite is available from the Harm Research Institute. It has different costs depending on whether it is to be used by students or organizations.

1.7.2 Routine Outcome Monitoring

Routine outcome monitoring (ROM) is important for assessing the clinical effectiveness of health services and for monitoring patient outcomes (Hall et al., 2013). Evidence-based ROM measures (e.g., psychometrically sound self-report questionnaires) can be used to supplement the structured and semi-structured diagnostic interviews described in Section 1.7.1, such as by assessing additional constructs associated with panic disorder and agoraphobia (e.g., problematic beliefs about panic, the extent to which certain physiological symptoms are feared), as well as for documenting objective changes occurring in these symptoms (in comparison with baseline symptom levels) over the course of treatment, in order to measure progress, evaluate treatment response and outcome, and determine what work remains to be done. It also allows for a more nuanced look at any target areas that may remain in patients who report more global improvements, such as that they have been experiencing fewer panic attacks and/or less intense panic symptoms, have started to fear the symptoms less, or have become less agoraphobic.

Fortunately, these questionnaires are typically brief (i.e., one to two pages), easy to administer (i.e., carefully worded instructions at the start, simply having to circle a number after each question, often available in electronic form, etc.), and have well-established norms derived from clinical trials to aid in assessing a particular patient's symptom severity relative to other individuals – be they "normal" controls in the community or other patients diagnosed with panic disorder and/or agoraphobia.

Commonly used routine outcome measures for panic disorder include the Agoraphobic Cognitions Questionnaire, the Body Sensations Questionnaire, the Agoraphobic Cognitions Scale, the Agoraphobic Self-Statements Questionnaire, the Albany Panic and Phobia Questionnaire, the Anxiety Sensitivity Index, the Anxiety Sensitivity Index-Revised 36, the Anxiety Sensitivity Profile, the Body Sensations Interpretation Questionnaire, the Body Vigilance Scale, the Mobility Inventory for Agoraphobia, the Panic and Agoraphobia Scale, the Panic Attack Questionnaire-Revised, the Panic Disorder Severity Scale – Self Report, the Phobic Avoidance Rating Scale, and the Texas Safety Maneuver Scale. An excellent resource that offers brief descriptions of these (and another 15 measures) is provided in a chapter entitled, "Measures for Panic Disorder and Agoraphobia" contained in the *Practitioner's Guide to Empirically Based Measures of Anxiety* (Antony, 2001).

2

Theories and Models

While a number of theories (e.g., genetic, biological, neurotransmitter, respiratory) have been proposed to explain both the etiology and perpetuation of panic disorder and agoraphobia, this chapter will focus on the two psychological theories that amassed the greatest empirical support: the cognitive model and the behavioral model. Together, they will be used to form the basis of the treatment program described in Chapter 4. It should be noted, however, that expert consensus statements propose that biological, psychological, and environmental factors all likely play a role (and often interact) to predispose an individual to experiencing panic, and then both to precipitate and perpetuate the cycle of panic attacks once they have started.

Biological, psychological, and environmental factors all play a role in panic disorder and agoraphobia

2.1 The Cognitive Model

The cognitive model (Clark, 1986; Clark, 1988; Clark et al., 1988; Salkovskis & Clark, 1986; Salkovskis, 1988; Salkovskis & Clark, 1990) proposes that panic attacks occur when individuals perceive certain somatic sensations as considerably more dangerous than they truly are, and then interpret their presence as a signal that they are about to experience a sudden and imminent disaster (i.e., a catastrophic misinterpretation of typically benign bodily sensations). For example, individuals may develop a panic attack if they misinterpret heart palpitations as being a sign of an impending heart attack, or if they misinterpret shortness of breath and/or smothering sensations as an indication that they will stop breathing and die, or if they misinterpret shaking or trembling as a sign they are losing control.

The bodily sensations that are most often catastrophically misinterpreted are typically those found in normal anxiety responses (e.g., heart palpitations, shortness of breath, dizziness) but may also include a wide range of other stimuli (e.g., visual floaters), emotions (e.g., anger, excitement), thoughts or images (e.g., the belief or image of going crazy based on moments when the mind suddenly goes blank), substances (e.g., caffeine or certain drugs), or activities (e.g., exercise or sex). In addition, for some patients the panic-triggering sensations and their interpretations of those sensations remain fairly constant across time, while for others both the sensations and interpretations change over time (Clark, 1986). Finally, the symptoms and presentation of panic may also vary according to the cultural background of the individual or cultural context in which it is occurring (Amering & Katschnig, 1990; Hofmann & Hinton, 2014).

The central tenet of the cognitive model is that, regardless of whether internal (e.g., a sensation, image, or thought) or external (e.g., agoraphobic situation), the common denominator across all trigger stimuli is that patients with panic disorder perceive them as threatening. As a result, Clark (1986) suggests that this perception of threat then generates a mild state of apprehension, which is accompanied by a wide range of somatic sensations. For patients with panic disorder, these sensations are then catastrophically misinterpreted, essentially creating a "vicious circle" in which individuals then experience an elevation in the perceived threatening nature of the situation, which causes a further increase in apprehension, which in turn causes a further elevation of the somatic sensations, which are then misinterpreted again as further "proof" of the impending catastrophe. This ultimately culminates in what patients describe as a full-symptom panic attack (see Figure 1).

It is important to note that the cognitive model can therefore be used to explain both panic attacks that are preceded by a period of heightened anxiety, as well as panic attacks that appear to come on "out of the blue." In the case of panic attacks that are preceded by a period of heightened anxiety, Clark (1986) notes that increased anxiety preceding the attack stems from the anticipation of experiencing a panic attack, such as when patients with panic disorder and agoraphobia experience an attack in a situation (e.g., a supermarket) in which they have previously panicked. In this case, Clark (1986) suggests that upon entering such a situation patients with a history of panic attacks develop anticipatory anxiety about experiencing another panic attack and, a result, selectively focus their attention inward (on their somatic functioning) in an attempt to monitor for any early warning signs of an impending attack, notice an unpleasant body sensation (ironically often generated by anticipatory anxiety and then noticed due to their hypervigilance), interpret

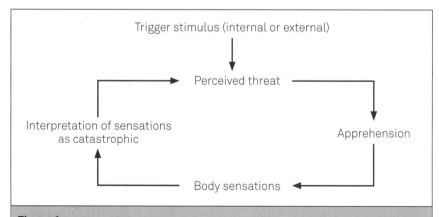

Figure 1
The cognitive model of panic attacks. Reprinted from *Behaviour Research and Therapy*, 24, D. M. Clark, A cognitive approach to panic, p. 463, © 1986, with permission from Elsevier.

this as "evidence" of an impending attack (i.e., perceive it as threatening), and consequently activate the vicious circle that produces the attack.

In cases in which panic attacks appear to come on out of the blue, Clark (1986) suggests that it is likely that heightened anxiety is also present; however, in these cases it is not due to the anticipation of a panic attack. For example, patients with panic disorder may become emotionally dysregulated during an interpersonal conflict, then notice the elevated somatic sensations caused by the conflict after it is over, fail to connect the sensations to the situation that caused them and instead catastrophically misinterpret these sensations, and consequently, once again, activate the vicious circle that produces an attack. In a similar fashion, the trigger for an out of the blue panic attack could be caused by any other high intensity emotional state (including positive emotions, such as excitement) or by some innocuous event, such as by suddenly getting up from the sitting position (dizziness), exercise (breathlessness, palpitations) or drinking coffee (palpitations).

In essence, patients with panic disorder often fail to distinguish between the triggering stimulus and the subsequent panic attack and so perceive the attacks as having no cause and coming out of the blue. According to Clark (1986), this is understandable given their general beliefs about the meaning of an attack (e.g., patients who believe that there is something wrong with their heart are unlikely to view a palpitation that triggers a panic attack as different from the panic attack itself, and instead are likely to view both as aspects of the same thing – a heart attack – or, as is often the case, a "near miss").

Support for the cognitive model of panic comes from the fact that patients with panic disorder report having thoughts of imminent danger (e.g., having a heart attack or going insane) during their panic attacks, and report that these thoughts typically occur after they notice specific body sensations (Hibbert, 1984). Additional evidence in support of the cognitive model of panic comes from the finding that laboratory-provoked attacks may lead to similar physiological sensations in patients with panic disorder versus normal controls, but only patients with panic disorder who catastrophically misinterpret these sensations will go on to develop panic attacks (Sanderson & Wetzler, 1990). Furthermore, following the administration of a panicogenic substance in the laboratory, individuals who declared themselves able to control the amount were less prone to panic attacks than individuals who felt they had no such control (Sanderson et al., 1989). Similarly, studies (e.g., Salkovskis et al., 1991) have demonstrated that panic attacks can be alleviated solely with cognitive techniques, such as cognitive restructuring, which attempts to challenge and substitute catastrophic misinterpretations of bodily sensations with more balanced rational thoughts, and that this change in catastrophic misinterpretations also predicts subsequent reductions in overall symptom severity, panic attack frequency, distress/apprehension, and avoidance behavior (Teachman et al., 2010).

2.2 The Behavioral Model

> About one person in four will experience at least one panic attack in their lifetime

The behavioral model of panic (e.g., Barlow, 2004; Bouton et al., 2001) conceptualizes the initial panic attack as a "false alarm" that occurs among the general population in the absence of any life-threatening trigger stimulus but often during a particularly stressful time (note: this can be negative stress, such as that caused by the loss of a job, or positive stress, such as that caused by a promotion at work or the birth of a child) and clearly at a much higher rate (e.g., in one study about 23% of people interviewed experienced at least one panic attack in their lifetime) than previously realized (Kessler et al., 2006). While occasional false alarms are common, most people who experience false alarms do not become apprehensive about having future panic attacks (i.e., only about 3% of the population will be diagnosed with panic disorder in their lifetime). This is in contrast with "true alarms" in which panic attacks are proposed to occur as an evolutionarily adaptive, automated ("fight or flight") response to a situation that is truly dangerous or life threatening to the individual, such as being attacked (e.g., centuries ago by a lion; nowadays by an attacker).

The behavioral model proposes that when the initial false alarm (spontaneous panic attack) occurs in certain individuals with a genetically based biological vulnerability (i.e., they are hardwired to respond to the stress of negative life events with exaggerated neurobiological activity) and/or psychological vulnerability (e.g., social learning at a young age to view unpredictable and uncontrollable events as potentially dangerous), it becomes associated with feeling of intense anxiety and danger and, via classical conditioning, so too become the somatic sensations (e.g., dizziness or palpitations) that the individual experienced during the initial false alarm. This association/conditioning then leads to the development of "learned alarms" in which individuals: (a) learn to become fearful of the somatic sensations because they believe that they will lead to another attack, (b) become increasingly anxious and apprehensive over having additional alarms or panic attacks in the future, and (c) ultimately go on to develop panic disorder. This is also known as the "fear-of-fear" cycle (see Figure 2). In addition, their predisposition to be somatically preoccupied becomes intensified as they focus even more attention on themselves, with the result being that they become even more sensitive to false alarms than they were when they first had their attack. Finally, behavioral models suggest that patients with panic disorder then develop a repertoire of avoidance, escape, and "safety" behaviors (shaped at least in part by cultural, social, and environmental factors), in an attempt to cope with the unexpected panic attacks and/or situations they fear will trigger them.

The behavioral model of panic has received empirical support from several sources (e.g., Barlow, 2004; Bouton et al., 2001). For example, a number of studies have found that many patients with panic disorder describe one or more negative life events as preceding their first panic attack, thus providing circumstantial evidence for the notion that the initial false alarm may result from an overreaction to life stress. In addition, there is clear evidence

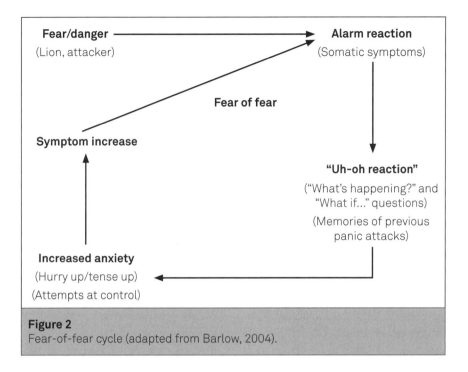

Figure 2
Fear-of-fear cycle (adapted from Barlow, 2004).

that somatic cues can become conditioned to anxiety – and that interoceptive exposure can weaken these learned associations – supporting the model's hypothesis that false alarms become associated with somatic sensations. Finally, patients with panic disorder have been found to exhibit a greater fear over somatic sensations than do patients with other psychiatric disorders and normal controls, thus supporting the notion that patients with panic disorder learn to become more apprehensive about somatic cues.

3

Diagnosis and Treatment Indications

Patients with panic disorder or agoraphobia are almost always treated as outpatients

This chapter provides a framework for the diagnostic assessment and treatment decision-making process for panic disorder and agoraphobia. It should be noted that the treatment of panic disorder and agoraphobia is generally conducted entirely on an outpatient basis, as the condition by itself rarely warrants hospitalization (APA, 2009). Fortunately, a range of specific psychological and pharmacological interventions have received strong empirical support in the treatment of panic disorder and agoraphobia, and a combination of the cognitive and behavioral models can be used as the foundation for assessing and conceptualizing a patient's symptoms and designing the treatment plan, as well as determining whether medication(s) should be considered, either instead of or to augment psychological treatment. Given the need to balance information gathering with rapport and alliance building, present evidence-based treatment options, familiarize the patient with a cognitive behavioral approach, and enhance motivation and commitment to change, this phase may take several sessions to complete. Factors to consider include the complexity of the patient's psychiatric history and symptomatology, clinical presentation, and comorbidity (including medical conditions and/or substance use disorders), age, gender, race, educational level, treatment history, treatment preference, access to expert care, insight into their problems, and readiness for change.

3.1 Diagnostic Assessment

Along with the evidence-based structured and semi-structured diagnostic interviews and evidence-based ROM measures that can be used to confirm the diagnosis of panic disorder as primary, and screen for any comorbid diagnoses and/or subthreshold syndromes, a cognitive-behaviorally focused diagnostic assessment typically involves asking the patient to provide a general description and history of their presenting problem and then focusing on the underlying situational factors and affective, cognitive, and behavioral components that appear to be connected to the origin and maintenance of the presenting problem.

In the case of panic disorder (with or without a separate diagnosis of agoraphobia), it can be particularly informative and helpful to have the patient describe: (a) the circumstances associated with their first panic attack (precipitating factors), (b) the typical panic attack symptoms the patient experiences (be alert for any culturally influenced expressions/explanations of panic, such as *ataque de nervios* within Puerto Rican culture, *khyâl* overload within Cambodian culture, *Pa Leng* within Chinese cultures), (c) any factors that the patient believes have been associated with exacerbations or ameliorations or cycling of their panic symptoms, and (d) any changes the patient has made (e.g., in how they think or what they do) in response to the panic attacks throughout the course of the disorder (perpetuating factors). Armed with this information, the clinician can then search for functional relationships between the panic attack cues (e.g., situations, somatic sensations) and any potentially problematic thoughts (e.g., overestimations of danger, catastrophizing, perceived inability to cope/function) and maladaptive coping behaviors (e.g., utilization of safety behaviors, modifications to lifestyle, and/or outright avoidances).

> Clinicians need to be sensitive to culture-bound symptoms, such as ataque de nervios, khyâl, and Pa Leng

As with all initial psychiatric diagnostic assessments, it is important to consider (and rule out) any *medical conditions* that may have predisposed the patient to panic attacks or precipitated the attacks, or that may perpetuate and/or exacerbate them. In fact, as mentioned earlier, a criterion found throughout the diagnostic criteria boxes in the DSM-5 is that if the psychiatric symptoms can be better accounted for by a medical condition (and/or substance use/abuse/withdrawal) a psychiatric diagnosis should *not* be given. Since the symptoms of a panic attack are similar to cardiac and pulmonary conditions and may also be caused by medical diseases such as thyroid disorders (e.g., hyperthyroidism), it is important to make sure the patient has recently had a thorough physical examination and receives medical clearance before proceeding with a psychological treatment (especially interoceptive and in vivo exposure). Typically, however, patients presenting with panic disorder will have often already sought multiple medical evaluations and, in many cases, will have also presented to an emergency room (ER) out of a fear of having a heart attack – and thus will most likely already have been cleared of any major medical issues. In fact, it is quite common for patients to be *referred* for psychological treatment after presenting to the ER and being informed that they are in good medical health and that their somatic symptoms, while real, are, in fact, being caused by anxiety.

> Patients with anxiety disorders have often been fully medically evaluated as a result of frequent visits to hospital emergency departments

3.2 Treatment Indications

3.2.1 Empirically Supported Treatments for Panic Disorder and Agoraphobia

A range of specific psychological and pharmacological interventions have received strong empirical support in the treatment of panic disorder. Currently, most reviews (e.g., Papola et al., 2022; Szuhany & Simon, 2022) and expert consensus treatment guidelines suggest that CBT, which includes techniques derived from both the cognitive and behavioral models, and pharmacotherapy (in particular SSRIs and SNRIs) be considered "first-line" treatments for panic disorder (with or without a separate diagnosis of agoraphobia). This section will briefly describe each, along with a summary of the advantages and disadvantages commonly noted with each of these treatment approaches, as applied to panic disorder and agoraphobia.

CBT for Panic Disorder and Agoraphobia

Consistent with the cognitive and behavioral models described in Chapter 2, CBT considers panic attacks through both a cognitive lens (misperception of an otherwise benign trigger as threatening along with a catastrophic misinterpretation of bodily sensations in biologically and psychologically vulnerable patients) and a behavioral lens (conditioned response of fear associated with the symptoms experienced during the panic attack). As such, CBT focuses on altering both cognitive and behavioral patterns that underlie and perpetuate panic disorder and agoraphobia. Patients are educated on the nature of panic disorder and agoraphobia via psychoeducation and self-monitoring and then are taught a set of cognitive and behavioral techniques that target both their fear of the panic attacks (with a particular focus on the somatic sensations associated with the attacks), as well as the recurring cycle of anticipatory anxiety, panic, and agoraphobic avoidance.

The cognitive techniques in CBT help patients identify, challenge, and modify dysfunctional beliefs (i.e., expectations) they hold about their panic symptoms (e.g., overestimating the probability that something bad will happen and/or catastrophizing how bad an outcome would be) as well as their perceived inability to cope and/or need to therefore utilize safety behaviors. The behavioral techniques in CBT help patients identify and reverse avoidance of panic-related cues and sensations through both interoceptive exposure (e.g., exposure to bodily sensations) and in vivo exposure (e.g., exposure to phobic situations), as well as create behavioral experiments for testing out (and ideally violating) expectancies. Treatment duration and outcome depend on symptom severity, psychological or biological comorbidities, readiness to change, ability to understand CBT concepts and master CBT skills, maintenance of skills following treatment, and the treatment provider's competence (Newman, 2000).

CBT is better tolerated, more cost-effective, and has lower relapse rates than pharmacological intervention

As is the case with pharmacotherapy, there are numerous advantages and disadvantages to CBT. Advantages of CBT include: (a) it is clinically effective, with findings of panic-free status achieved in approximately 70–90% of patients and rates of clinically significant improvement found to be 38–79%, depending on the criteria used; (b) the treatment tends to be fairly brief, typically lasting 12–20 sessions; and (c) the data suggest a long-term maintenance of treatment gains with low relapse rates after CBT is discontinued (i.e., durability), though more high-quality randomized clinical trials with 12 months or more of follow-up and reported relapse rates are needed (van Dis et al., 2020). In addition, relative to pharmacologic interventions, CBT appears to be better tolerated, more cost effective, and has lower relapse rates (Otto et al., 2000).

The disadvantages of CBT include the following: (a) the patient must have the time, motivation, and commitment to work hard – especially between sessions – in order to achieve improvement; (b) the treatment can be uncomfortable for many patients (especially initially), as it involves purposely reversing avoidance and resisting use of safety behaviors, while also provoking anxiety during interoceptive and in vivo exposure; (c) the structured nature of CBT may make it unsuitable for patients with more complex mental health needs or learning difficulties; and (d) the treatment is still not widely available (i.e., it is difficult to find a therapist trained to do CBT competently). Thus, to benefit from CBT, patients need to commit themselves to the process. The clinician can offer help and advice but cannot successfully treat the disorder without the patient's cooperation.

Pharmacotherapy for Panic Disorder and Agoraphobia

Consistent with the hypothesis that a dysfunction of brain pathways (Ninan & Dunlop, 2005), using γ-aminobutyric acid (Zwanzger & Rupprecht, 2005), serotonin (Maron & Shlik, 2006), and noradrenaline (Neumeister et al., 2005) as neurotransmitters, is involved in the pathogenesis of panic disorder, the efficacy of antipanic drugs is probably mediated by their effects on these neurochemical systems, even though their exact mechanism remains unclear (Marchesi, 2008). These agents are believed to reduce panic attack frequency by increasing the concentration of serotonin in the brain. On average, first-line medication trials report response rates between 70% and 80% and remission rates of approximately 45% during the acute treatment of panic disorder.

The APA's *Practice Guideline for the Treatment of Patients With Panic Disorder* (2009, p. 13) states that, "SSRIs, SNRIs, TCAs [tricyclic antidepressants, and benzodiazepines have demonstrated efficacy in numerous controlled trials and are recommended for treatment of panic disorder." The guideline also notes:

> Because SSRIs, SNRIs, TCAs, and benzodiazepines appear roughly comparable in their efficacy for panic disorder, selecting a medication for a particular patient mainly involves considerations of side effects (including any applicable warnings from the U.S. Food and Drug Administration [FDA]), cost, pharmacological properties, potential drug interactions, prior treatment history, co-occurring general medical and psychiatric conditions, and the strength of the evidence base for the particular medication in treatment of panic disorder.

In addition, the guideline notes, "The relatively favorable safety and side effect profile of SSRIs and SNRIs makes them the best initial choice for many patients with panic disorder," and adds that, "Although TCAs are effective, the side effects and greater toxicity in overdose associated with them often limit their acceptability to patients and their clinical utility."

Finally, the guideline notes that "SSRIs, SNRIs, and TCAs are all preferable to benzodiazepines as monotherapies for patients with co-occurring

SSRIs and SNRIs are generally preferable to TCAs and benzodiazepines in the treatment of panic disorder

depression or substance use disorders." In fact, given the prevalence with which benzodiazepines are often prescribed for anxiety disorders in general, and panic disorder specifically, it is important to note that the APA's *Practice Guideline for the Treatment of Patients With Panic Disorder* also states that while,

> Benzodiazepines may be especially useful adjunctively with antidepressants to treat residual anxiety symptoms ... and may be preferred (as monotherapies or in combination with antidepressants) for patients with very distressing or impairing symptoms in whom rapid symptom control is critical ... the benefit of more rapid response to benzodiazepines must be balanced against the possibilities of troublesome side effects (e.g., sedation) and physiological dependence that may lead to difficulty discontinuing the medication. (p. 13)

On the other hand, the World Federation of Societies of Biological Psychiatry guidelines recommend the SSRIs (citalopram, escitalopram, fluoxetine, sertraline, fluvoxamine, paroxetine) and the SNRI venlafaxine as the first-line treatments for panic disorder. In these guidelines, TCAs (imipramine and clomipramine), benzodiazepines (alprazolam, clonazepam, lorazepam, and diazepam), and the monoamine oxidase inhibitor phenelzine were all considered second-line treatments due to their associated side-effects profiles (Bandelow et al., 2008). Of note, these guidelines (p. 267) also state, "A combination of CBT and medication is more effective than the monotherapies."

Table 1 (taken from Batelaan et al., 2012) displays the generic names, starting doses, mean therapeutic doses, and maximum doses of medications with demonstrated clinical efficacy for panic disorder and agoraphobia. A similar table (Table VI, p. 261), noting the recommended daily dose range of medications (for adults) with demonstrated clinical efficacy for panic disorder and agoraphobia, can also be found in Bandelow et al. (2008).

Reviewing the various advantages and disadvantages of using a medication with the patient is an important part of a thorough informed consent to treatment process, even in cases in which the clinician will not be the one prescribing the medication. Advantages of medications include: (a) they are relatively safe and easy to use, (b) they are relatively easy to access, and (c) they are clinically effective, with panic-free rates at the end of active treatment ranging from 54% to 61% (compared with 35% for placebo). In addition, approximately 75% of patients given the active treatment (as opposed to placebo) in research trials have been considered responders, with nearly 45% achieving remission. Disadvantages of medications include: (a) the possibility of side effects, (b) they often must be continued to be taken in order to sustain the gains made in treatment, and (c) their long-term cost (to both the patient and health-care system) can be higher than a time-limited, short-term psychological treatments such as CBT.

Table 1
Dosage of Drugs Effective in Panic Disorder

Drug name	Start (mg/day)	Mean (mg/day)	Maximum (mg/day)
Antidepressants			
SSRIs			
Citalopram	10	20–30	60
Escitalopram	5	10	20
Fluoxetine	20	20	60
Fluvoxamine	50	100–150	300
Paroxetine	10	20–40	60
Sertraline	50	100	200
SNRIs			
Venlafaxine	37.5	75–150	225
TCAs			
Clomipramine	25	100–150	250
Imipramine	25	100–150	300
Benzodiazepines			
Alprazolam	1.5	4–6	*
Clonazepam	1	2–3	*
Diazepam	5–10	40–50	*
Lorazepam	1	2–4 *	*
Monoamine oxidase inhibitors			
Phenelzine	10	40–60	*

Note. *Only use mean dosage. Reprinted from *International Journal of Neuropsychopharmacology*, 15, N. M. Batelaan, A. J. Van Balkom, & D. J. Stein, Evidence-based pharmacotherapy of panic disorder: An update, p. 405, © 2012, with permission from Oxford University Press.

Table 2 (taken from Marchesi, 2008) summarizes the relative advantages and disadvantages of pharmacotherapy and CBT in the treatment of panic disorder.

Table 2
Advantages and Disadvantages of Pharmacotherapy and CBT in the Treatment of Panic Disorder

Advantage/Disadvantage	Pharmacotherapy	CBT
Side effects	++	0
Rapid onset of action	++*	+
Efficacy on more severe panic attacks and anticipatory anxiety	++	+
Efficacy on phobic avoidance	+	++
Efficacy on severe depression	++§	+
Persistence of effect after stopping treatment	0	+
Use in primary care setting	++	0
Used by experienced therapists	+	++
Need to perform "homework" or to confront feared situations	0	++

Note. Particularly *benzodiazepines or §antidepressants. Reprinted from *Neuropsychiatric Disease and Treatment*, 4, C. Marchesi, Pharmacological management of panic disorder, © 2008, with permission from Dove Medical Press.

3.3 Factors That Influence Treatment Decisions

This section considers factors that influence clinical decisions regarding which type of treatment to recommend for a particular patient with panic disorder and agoraphobia.

3.3.1 Age

CBT for children under 7 years of age should be adapted to include parents

While CBT is considered to be the psychological treatment of choice for panic disorder (with or without a separate diagnosis of agoraphobia) in adults, the controlled evaluation of treatments for early childhood anxiety and related problems has been a relatively recent area of investigation, and, accordingly, trials examining early childhood anxiety treatment have not been well represented in existing systematic reviews of youth anxiety treatments (Comer et al., 2019). For example, a review by Higa-McMillan et al. (2016) found that only six treatments reached well-established status for child and adolescent anxiety, with their findings suggesting substantial support for CBT as an effective and appropriate first-line treatment for youth with anxiety disorders. In accordance with this, in the first randomized controlled trial to evaluate the feasibility and efficacy of panic control treatment for adolescents ages

14 to 17 years, Pincus et al. (2010) found a significant reduction in clinician-rated severity of panic disorder and in self-reported anxiety, anxiety sensitivity, and depression, in comparison to control group participants, and noted that these treatment gains were maintained at 3- and 6-month follow-up. Children younger than 7 years old typically do not possess the developmental abilities needed to understand and apply cognitive behavioral strategies to their symptoms, but CBT has been adapted for delivery to parents of children with anxiety disorders, or to parents and children together (Alvarez et al., 2021).

In general, expert consensus guidelines suggest starting with CBT for milder cases, and then augmenting with medication as the severity and/or comorbidity increase, while also considering factors such as patient preference and access to expert care. One study by Hazlett-Stevens et al. (2002) examining predictors of willingness to consider medication and psychosocial treatment for panic disorder in patients in primary care settings found that willingness to consider medication treatment for panic disorder was associated with older age; however, the potential vulnerability to side effects and interactions with other medications should be assessed when considering medications in the elderly. In addition, a recent systematic review of pharmacological approaches in the management of panic disorder in older patients (Caldirola et al., 2023) concluded that the pharmacological management of panic disorder in older patients has received virtually no attention, adding that findings are scant, dated, and affected by methodological flaws and, thus, do not provide significant advances in our understanding of whether some recommended medications may be superior to others, as well as the optimal doses to maximize their clinical effectiveness and tolerability in this age group.

Elderly patients may be more vulnerable to the side effects of medications prescribed for panic disorder or agoraphobia

3.3.2 Gender

While panic disorder is 2.5 times more prevalent among women than men, Starcevic et al. (2007) found that both females and males did not differ significantly in terms of their tendency to anticipate catastrophic consequences of panic, before or after CBT-based treatment. In addition, they found that for both females and males, the tendency to make catastrophic appraisals decreased significantly with treatment. Thus, they concluded that the apparently higher risk of panic recurrence in women does not seem to be related to their panic-related catastrophic appraisals. In addition, their findings also supported the notion that there is no gender difference in response to CBT-based treatment of patients with panic disorder and agoraphobia. In addition, despite numerous studies, few consistently replicable differences have been found between females and males in panic disorder phenomenology, course of illness, or treatment responsivity (APA, 2009) – be it CBT or medications. In terms of medications, however, factors such as the sexual side-effect profile should be considered, as only about 25% of patients who experience sexual dysfunction as a result of medication report being able to tolerate

Panic disorder is more than twice as prevalent among women

this side effect (Montejo-Gonzalez et al., 1997). For females, pregnancy and breastfeeding status should also be considered, as practice guidelines (e.g., APA, 2009) suggest that psychosocial interventions should be used in lieu of pharmacotherapy for women with panic disorder who are pregnant, nursing, or planning to become pregnant.

3.3.3 Race

A study by Hazlett-Stevens et al. (2002) examining predictors of willingness to consider medication and psychosocial treatment for panic disorder in patients in primary care settings found that Asian and African American/Black patients were less likely than White American patients to indicate willingness to consider medication treatment for panic disorder. However, this finding is in contrast with other studies (e.g., Cooper-Patrick et al., 1997; Lee et al., 2021) that have found that members of minority groups are less willing to consider psychological treatments and prefer medications, due to ongoing concerns about the stigma attached to receiving psychotherapy. Despite these differences in willingness, however, the data suggest that many minority patients with panic disorder and agoraphobia achieve clinically significant improvement with CBT.

3.3.4 Educational Level

Patients with lower levels of education are more likely to drop out of CBT

According to Keijsers et al. (2001), lower levels of education have been fairly consistently associated with a higher dropout risk – both in the general psychotherapy literature, as well as in several CBT studies on affective disorders. This makes particular sense in the case of CBT, as CBT relies on psychoeducation and the teaching of new skills, and those skills must be practiced between sessions if they are to work. As such, recent studies have focused on the role of memory and learning as essential ingredients for therapeutic success and neurobiological processes related to learning have been related to the success of psychological treatments (Bruijniks et al., 2019). As these tasks may be difficult for patients who are more limited or concrete in their thinking (e.g., developmentally disabled and cognitively impaired patients), medication is often recommended. Interestingly, one study (Hazlett-Stevens et al., 2002) examining predictors of willingness to consider medication and psychosocial treatment for panic disorder found that willingness to consider medication treatment for panic disorder was associated with *lower* education – although the authors note that this somewhat unexpected finding (they had predicted based on the available utilization research findings that lower education level would be associated with less willingness to consider either type of treatment) may have been affected by the overall high education level of the sample.

3.3.5 Individual Preference

Individual preference for the type of treatment is a core component of evidence-based mental health care and has been shown to impact treatment retention and outcome, as greater adherence to either treatment (especially CBT) can be expected from patients who agree willingly to a treatment plan that is presented in a collaborative manner as opposed to situations in which the treatment is unilaterally presented and forced upon the patient. A 2013 meta-analysis of 34 studies spanning primary and specialty care settings as well as nontreatment-seeking samples provided evidence that adults were 3 times more likely to express a preference for psychological treatment to pharmacological treatment for anxiety disorders (McHugh et al., 2013). This led the authors to suggest that consideration of patient preference, along with treatment efficacy and clinical expertise, may be important to optimizing outcomes in clinical settings. Given the comparable efficacy of CBT and medications, along with the fact that patient preference is associated with fewer treatment dropouts and increased therapeutic alliance (Windle et al., 2020), as well as more positive treatment outcomes (Swift et al., 2019), reviewing the relative advantages and disadvantages of CBT versus medications should allow the patient to make an informed decision about which treatment they would prefer to receive and, in so doing, enhance the outcome of whichever treatment is ultimately selected.

> Most adults prefer psychological treatment to pharmacological treatment for anxiety disorders

3.3.6 Social Support

A study by Jakubovski and Bloch (2016) examining anxiety-disorder-specific predictors of treatment outcome found that limited social support was associated with poor treatment outcome, regardless of whether the treatment assignment was medications or CBT. Relatedly, this study, along with previous studies, have found that improved social support has been associated with treatment success for CBT in social phobia (Mersch et al., 1991) and PTSD (Thrasher et al., 2010). It should be noted, however, that many studies look at *perceived* social supports, which by definition implies that the mere presence of loved ones or close friends is inadequate as these only represent *potential* social supports during treatment. The challenge is to assess whether the people the patient identifies as potential social supports will actually be able to provide the appropriate level and type of support, guidance, and feedback to the patient – acting more like a coach than a therapist or drill sergeant. Qualities associated with a successful social support include being involved, available, empathic, and supportive as well as knowledgeable of the problem and model of treatment that is being used to address it, while also being firm and encouraging the patient to utilize the skills being learned in treatment and/or to be adherent with their medication. Patients who are emotionally overinvolved, impatient, or hostile, or inconsistent in their availability and support may actually have a deleterious impact on treatment outcome.

> Social support can dramatically affect the outcomes of treatment

3.3.7 Clinical Presentation and Comorbidity

Patients with panic disorder have significantly increased odds of being diagnosed with a comorbid disorder, including another anxiety or related disorder, mood disorder (especially major depressive disorder), impulse-control disorder, or substance use disorder (Bystritsky et al., 2010). Panic disorder is also more prevalent in patients with medical conditions (e.g., thyroid disease, chronic pain, and cardiac disease, as well as allergic and respiratory diseases) and the presence of medical comorbidity is associated with greater severity of panic disorder symptoms and disability (Meuret et al., 2017). Fortunately, the robust nature of CBT and medications often allows both approaches to simultaneously target the symptoms of panic disorder, agoraphobia, and other comorbid disorders, and, in general, the data clearly support CBT alone and medication alone as initial treatments for panic disorder. Interestingly, the data also suggest that the combination of CBT and medication confers little additional advantage over either alone, and that CBT does not appear as durable (i.e., does not seem to protect as well against relapse) when it is combined with medications.

> Substance abuse significantly impairs a client's ability to benefit from CBT

CBT alone, however, may be insufficient in patients with comorbid moderate-to-severe major depression, in those with severe, frequent panic attacks, rapid worsening of agoraphobia, and/or suicidal ideation, as well as in situations in which one might consider initial rescue treatment with a benzodiazepine to minimize or stop the panic attacks while waiting the 4–12 weeks for the first-line pharmacotherapy to become effective (Katzman et al., 2014). In addition, some patients may not be motivated to participate in CBT or may be too fearful to engage in any kind of exposure before first being treated with a medication. CBT alone may also be insufficient in patients presenting with conditions causing alterations in their perception, cognition, and/or judgment (e.g., psychotic and manic symptoms), as well as in patients who are actively abusing psychoactive substances (including benzodiazepines), as these conditions have been shown to impede the ability of patients to benefit from CBT exercises and may also reduce adherence. Conversely, despite having had a good response to medication for their panic attacks, some patients may still experience ongoing agoraphobic distress and/or avoidance and would therefore benefit from engaging in CBT-based exposure exercises. In addition, some patients may not want to take a medication due to concerns about potential side effects, previous negative experiences, or other medical issues. Finally, some researchers have suggested that CBT and medication outcomes may both be adversely impacted by the presence of various personality disorders, in particular Cluster C personality disorders (characterized by anxious, fearful thinking or behavior), which include avoidant personality disorder, dependent personality disorder, and obsessive-compulsive personality disorder. The data here are inconsistent, however, with some researchers suggesting that personality disorders are likely to predict poor treatment outcomes, and others concluding that they did not affect treatment outcome. Finally, it should also be noted that at times the overall symptom severity or lack of response to the standard forms of treatment may require a more intense regimen of whatever treatment is offered (i.e., a higher dose of medicine or more frequent CBT sessions).

3.3.8 Insight and Motivation

Patients with poor insight into the cause and nature of their panic attacks and/or low motivation to engage in the treatment exercises (e.g., interoceptive and in vivo exposure) typically have an attenuated response to CBT. While CBT is still worth attempting, an initial phase (e.g., one to four sessions) of motivational enhancement therapy or motivational interviewing may be necessary to help motivate patients resolve their ambivalence about engaging in treatment. Motivational enhancement therapy focuses on increasing intrinsic motivation by raising a patient's awareness of their problem, addressing any self-defeating thoughts about their problem, and increasing their confidence and their ability to change. In addition, in cases where the patient is not motivated to engage in CBT, beginning with medication may prove helpful.

Starting treatment with medication may be necessary when dealing with clients who are not motivated

3.3.9 Patient's Treatment History

Unfortunately, many patients with panic disorder (with or without a separate diagnosis of agoraphobia) have experienced only a partial response to treatment (be it medication or CBT), and others relapse even after achieving symptom remission during acute treatment. For patients who remain symptomatic after initial first-line treatment, reconsideration of the diagnosis, intensity of treatment (dose and duration of treatment), adherence, and initially overlooked psychiatric and medical comorbidities may be necessary. Unrecognized substance abuse should also be considered. If none of these are helpful, the clinician should employ a differential diagnostic approach to the component(s) of the panic disorder, such as concurrent psychosocial stressors, and related complications that have not responded, including panic attacks, phobic avoidance, anticipatory anxiety, and cognitive factors within the patient (Holt & Lydiard, 2007). If this proves unhelpful, the clinician should consider switching to (or augmenting with) a different first-line treatment (i.e., if starting with CBT, considering switching to, or adding, medication and vice versa). Ultimately, determining which treatment option to pursue at each stage is done collaboratively, using a transparent shared decision-making process between the patient and the clinician. A suggested algorithm (adapted from Ham et al., 2005) for the treatment of panic disorder is outlined in Figure 3.

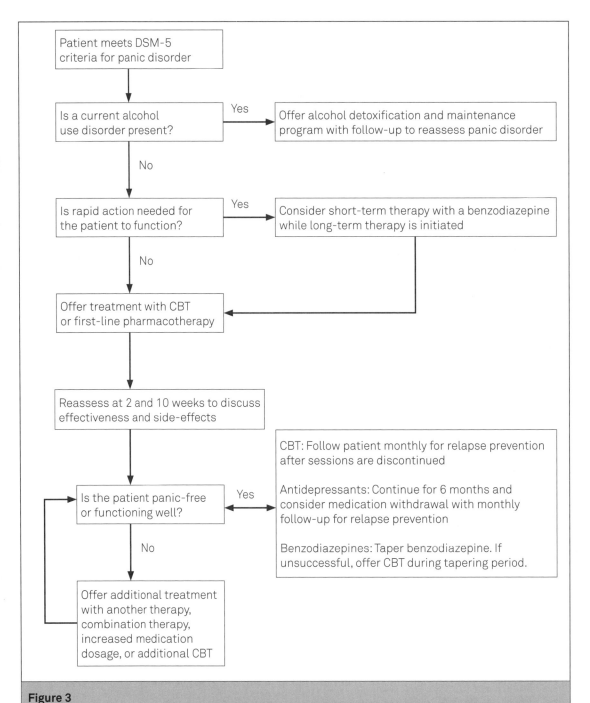

Figure 3
Algorithm for the treatment of panic disorder. Adapted from *American Family Physician*, 71, P. Ham, D. B. Waters, & M. N. Oliver, Treatment of panic disorder, © 2005, with permission from American Academy of Family Physicians. All Rights Reserved.

4

Treatment

The treatment of panic disorder and agoraphobia can generally be conducted entirely on an outpatient basis (APA, 2009), and there is strong empirical support for the use of psychological and/or pharmacological interventions in treatment of panic disorder in outpatient settings. This chapter presents a detailed description of how to plan and implement a comprehensive CBT program for patients presenting with the primary diagnosis of panic disorder with or without a separate diagnosis of agoraphobia. As detailed in Chapter 2, a combination of cognitive and behavioral models can be used as the foundation for determining how information about the patient's symptoms are assessed and conceptualized and how the initial treatment plan is designed. However, these symptoms should then be placed in the context of a host of additional factors (e.g., complexity, comorbidity, age, educational level, insight, treatment preference) when determining whether medication should be considered – either instead of or to augment the CBT program.

Table 3 shows a sample schedule, highlighting the key task for each treatment session. In an ideal situation, this treatment program would be completed in 12 sessions delivered over 16 weeks – with the first 10 sessions occurring weekly, the 11th session occurring 2 weeks after the 10th session, and the 12th session occurring 4 weeks after the 11th session. It should be noted, however, that in the interest of flexibility, the focus of this chapter is on assisting the patient to achieve mastery of particular skills in a more "modular" fashion, rather than on promoting a strict session-by-session protocol. Some patients have more complicated life histories, clinical presentations, and environmental and psychosocial stressors to contend with while also attempting to address their panic attacks. In addition, motivation and commitment are not static, but, rather, can wax and wane dynamically throughout the treatment, and may therefore need to be readdressed at various points. In other words, the clinician is encouraged to practice "flexibility within fidelity" (Kendall et al., 2008) while implementing this CBT program. Finally, depending on the patient's response to the program and symptom severity at the end of treatment, the clinician may opt to add one to three maintenance (i.e., "booster") sessions after the formal treatment program is terminated, to ensure maintenance of gains (via motivational enhancement strategies) and/or prevent relapse. If this is the case, the sessions can be scheduled at 1, 2, or 3 months after each previous session.

> A combination of cognitive and behavioral approaches often results in optimal outcomes

Twelve outpatient sessions are typically sufficient for treating panic disorder and agoraphobia

Table 3
Sample 12-Session Treatment Schedule

Session number	Key task(s)
Session 1	Diagnostic assessment Structured/semi-structured diagnostic assessment tool ROM measures (repeat each session)
Session 2	Presentation of the principles of CBT Presentation of the general CBT model Presentation of the CBT models of panic Tailoring CBT models of panic via a functional assessment
Session 3	Psychoeducation, motivation, commitment
Session 4	Rationale for interoceptive exposure, interoceptive exposure
Session 5	Interoceptive exposure, cognitive restructuring
Session 6	Interoceptive exposure, cognitive restructuring
Session 7	Interoceptive exposure, cognitive restructuring
Session 8	Rationale for interoceptive exposure, in vivo exposure, cognitive restructuring
Session 9	In vivo exposure, cognitive restructuring
Session 10	In vivo exposure, cognitive restructuring
Session 11	In vivo exposure, cognitive restructuring
Session 12	Relapse prevention, termination
Optional	
Booster 1	Relapse prevention, motivational enhancement
Booster 2	Relapse prevention, motivational enhancement
Booster 3	Relapse prevention, motivational enhancement

4.1 The Diagnostic Assessment

As is the case with every initial intake evaluation, a cognitive-behaviorally focused diagnostic interview begins by asking the patient to provide a general description of their problem (with an emphasis on identifying the affective, cognitive, and behavioral components), as well as current symptom severity and the reasons why they chose to seek help now. The clinician should also obtain a history of the present illness, including details surrounding its onset and, in particular, the circumstances associated with the first panic attack (precipitating factors) and the course of the disorder (perpetuating factors). While examining the course of the disorder, the clinician should inquire about any factors that the patient believes may have been associated with exacerbations or ameliorations or cycling of their panic symptoms. In addition, a detailed review of the patient's psychiatric (inpatient and outpatient and pharmacological) treatment history, particularly for panic disorder and agoraphobia, as well as the patient's medical (current and past), social (including educational, work, and relational), and substance use (alcohol, recreational drugs, use of medications outside of how they were prescribed, tobacco, caffeine) histories should be conducted. Diet and exercise, as well as sleep habits, should also be reviewed. Finally, the patient's family medical and psychiatric history (particularly as they relate to the primary diagnosis) should also be obtained (predisposing factors).

The clinician should be sure to specifically review all common symptoms of panic (e.g., heart racing and/or pounding, hot flash and/or sweating, trembling or shaking, shortness of breath, chest pain, dizziness/lightheadedness/faintness), while also being alert for any culturally influenced expressions/explanations of panic. The clinician should then search for functional relationships between the panic attack symptoms and any potentially problematic thoughts (e.g., overestimations of danger, catastrophizing, perceived inability to cope/function) and maladaptive behaviors (e.g., safety behaviors or outright avoidances).

Finally, the clinician should consider using a structured or semi-structured evidence-based diagnostic assessment tool such as the SCID, ADIS, or MINI, along with a packet of empirically based, psychometrically sound, ROM measures, to assess the patient's psychopathology and quality of life. This will allow the clinician to: (a) confirm the patient meets diagnostic criteria for panic disorder and/or agoraphobia, (b) screen for/rule out any comorbid diagnoses and/or subthreshold syndromes, and (c) gather additional objective data on the various constructs associated with panic disorder and/or agoraphobia (e.g., frequency of panic attacks, problematic beliefs about panic symptoms, the extent to which certain physiological symptoms are feared, agoraphobic avoidance) and their impact on the patient's quality of life enjoyment and satisfaction. Together, these can then be used to: (a) ascertain the initial severity of the patient's panic disorder and/or agoraphobia, (b) account for comorbidity in conceptualizing and treatment planning, (c) rule out other psychiatric disorders that may be primary causes of the panic attacks, and, in the case of the ROMs, (d) objectively assess for changes occurring in baseline symptom levels over the course of treatment in order to evaluate treatment response, measure progress, and determine any work remaining in treatment.

As with all initial diagnostic evaluations, it is important to consider (and rule out) the role that any medical conditions may be playing on the etiology, perpetuation, and exacerbation of psychiatric illnesses. This phase may take several sessions to complete, depending on the complexity of the patient's psychiatric history and symptomatology, their insight into their problems,

4.2 Methods of Treatment

4.2.1 Presentation of the Principles of CBT and General CBT Model

CBT focuses on how the symptoms of panic disorder are currently being perpetuated (rather than precipitating factors)

Research (e.g., King & Boswell, 2019) suggests that introducing certain research-supported techniques and strategies in the first sessions of CBT can positively initiate the therapeutic process. Therefore, before utilizing any cognitive or behavioral interventions, it is important to invest some time upfront presenting the core principles of CBT that distinguish it from other psychotherapy approaches, providing an overview of the general model CBT, providing the rationale and goal-oriented framework, and, in general, cultivating an attitude of collaborative empiricism. This way, the clinician can ensure the patient understands how CBT works and, more importantly, what will be expected from them in order to make the treatment a success.

In general, CBT places relatively less of an emphasis on *predisposing* and *precipitating* factors and instead focuses much more on how the symptoms of panic disorder are currently being *perpetuated* (as what causes and what maintains a disorder are often two very different mechanisms). As such, the focus of CBT sessions is much more on the present (though some time may be spent detailing the precipitating factors surrounding the initial panic attack) and much less on the distal past and early childhood events – unless some explicit connection between them appears likely.

The *transtheoretical* components of CBT for panic disorder typically include psychoeducation, interoceptive exposure, in vivo exposure, and cognitive therapy. The *psychoeducation* component of CBT for panic disorder involves socializing the patient to the general cognitive behavioral model, normalizing panic attacks by providing psychoeducation on their prevalence and explaining the cause of each of the panic symptoms, and then providing a rationale for how the treatment techniques are designed to weaken the associations between the somatic symptoms and the anxiety, apprehension, and avoidance tendencies that they generate.

Interoceptive exposure involves having patients engage in activities (e.g., rapidly climbing stairs, breathing through a straw, voluntarily hyperventilating) that allow them to gradually and systematically confront internal physiological sensations that are feared (and therefore typically avoided). *In vivo exposure* entails confronting real-life situations that typically evoke the fear of panic attacks.

Interoceptive exposure and in vivo exposure are then often combined with *cognitive therapy* interventions that focus on having patients predict feared consequences while doing the exposure and then creating ways to test them and violate expectations. For example, a patient who fears going out into a crowded supermarket because they believe that they will have a panic attack will be required to remain in the middle of a crowded grocery store during a peak time until the associated distress decreases on its own, without attempting to reduce the distress by withdrawing from the situation or performing any safety behaviors. In addition, the patient may also be asked to predict – along with a rating of their confidence in their prediction – what would happen if they did have a panic attack (e.g., they might fear that they will embarrass or humiliate themselves in some way), and then create an objective way to assess whether their prediction was accurate and how confident they were in it afterwards.

It is important to note that CBT is meant to be brief (i.e., much shorter than more traditional forms of psychotherapy) and, ideally, time limited (i.e., agree up front on a fixed number of sessions, which can be extended if necessary). As such, the clinician and patient collaborate to set an agenda for each session that is structured and connected to the goals of the treatment (which are determined near the end of the initial phase). In addition, CBT relies on active collaboration in which the clinician and patient both take a scientific approach to understanding and addressing the patient's symptoms ("collaborative empiricism"), is skills based, includes homework exercises, and has a goal of helping patients to "become their own therapist" by the end of the treatment. Finally, in CBT it is assumed that there will often be some symptoms remaining at the end of treatment and that even after a successful course of treatment the symptoms will likely return. Therefore, in CBT, relapse prevention strategies (including a plan to continue practicing the skills learned) are built into the last phase of treatment in order to minimize the risk of relapse if and when any symptoms return after termination.

> By design, CBT is brief and time limited, and includes relapse prevention strategies

After presenting the principles of CBT, answering any questions the patient may have, and making sure they have the time, motivation, and commitment necessary to start to work on their panic disorder, one additional key component in CBT involves providing the patient with an overview of the general CBT model (Fenn & Byrne, 2013). The goal here is to emphasize that CBT is based on a well-established theoretical model that suggests that all situations we experience can be broken down into the three major modalities: feelings, actions, and thoughts. The CBT model proposes that each of these three modalities is equally important, and each modality is inextricably interconnected with the other two. Based on this notion, CBT capitalizes on the relationships that exist between feelings, actions, and thoughts to help patients cope better with aversive stimuli (e.g., feeling anxious or depressed). In other words, CBT proposes that the best way to improve how you *feel* is to change how you *think* and change how you *act*. Note that the CBT model does not ignore the patient's feelings (a myth about CBT), but rather acknowledges the challenge of producing emotional change directly and proposes that improvements in emotional processing are often incidental rather than focal (Baker et al., 2012). Instead, in CBT the clinician chooses to target the patient's thoughts and actions, with the belief that each influences feelings.

> CBT clinicians do not ignore emotions, but consider improvements in them to be a byproduct of changes in thoughts and behaviors

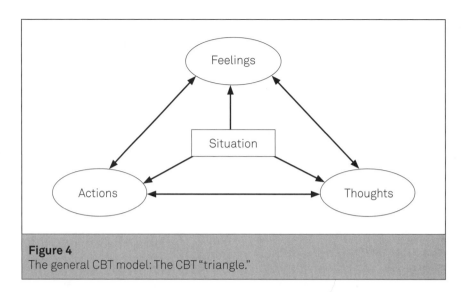

Figure 4
The general CBT model: The CBT "triangle."

Describing the CBT triangle helps clients understand the theoretical rationale for therapy

Finally, for many patients, providing a visual illustration of the general CBT model through a drawing of the CBT "triangle" (Figure 4) can be helpful. When illustrating the CBT triangle, it is often helpful to: (a) provide the information using an interactive/Socratic style, (b) convert the model into a formulation by demonstrating how the general model can be used to explain specific examples from the patient's life, and (c) give a blank copy of the model to the patient to review/complete for themselves as the clinician guides them through it. Be sure to answer any questions the patient may have about it before moving on.

Presentation of the CBT Models of Panic

Presenting a conceptual model for CBT will help your patient understand the rationale for exposure therapy

In theory, panic attacks are often conceptualized using either a cognitive perspective (misperception of an otherwise benign trigger as threatening along with a catastrophic misinterpretation of bodily sensations in biologically and psychologically vulnerable patients) or a behavioral perspective (conditioned response of fear associated with the symptoms experienced during the panic attack). In practice, however, most clinicians combine the two when conceptualizing and treating patients. As such, after providing an overview of the general model CBT, the clinician can then illustrate to the patient how it can be modified to explain why the patient has been experiencing recurrent panic attacks, using both cognitive and behavioral models. As was the case when describing the CBT triangle, it is often helpful to: (a) provide the information using an interactive/Socratic style, (b) tailor the cognitive and behavioral models to the patient using a functional assessment, and (c) give a blank copy of each of the models (see Figure 1 and Figure 2 in Chapter 2) to the patient to review/complete for themselves as the clinician guides them through each of them. Points of overlap between the two models should be noted, and an explanation of how CBT will address the problematic thought and behavioral patterns found in each model should be given. Finally, the clinician should note that most expert consensus statements suggest that biological, psychological, and environmental factors all likely play a role (and often interact) in generating and perpetuating panic attacks, with this CBT program focusing on the psychological and environmental factors and the other first-line treatment (i.e., medications) focusing more directly on the biological factors (e.g., neurotransmitters). Answer any questions the patient may have before moving on.

Tailoring the Models Using a Functional Assessment
The functional assessment involves the collection of highly detailed, patient-specific information about the triggers for panic attacks and the patient's cognitive and behavioral responses to these triggers. As such, it should include a complete description of all their catastrophic cognitions as well as their patterns of escape and avoidance, and any "safety behaviors" employed (which may be both cognitive and behavioral). A blank copy of either or both models can be used to capture and organize all the pertinent information in a simplified and easy to understand conceptualization of the problem and can then also be used as a basis for the CBT program to follow.

Begin by providing a rationale to the patient for doing a detailed functional assessment of their panic symptoms. The rationale should include the following points: (1) CBT involves learning skills to weaken the connection between panic responses to physiological sensations and agoraphobic situations; (2) in order to tailor the program to the patient's specific panic-related thoughts, sensations, and behaviors, the clinician (and patient) must have as thorough an understanding as possible of the symptoms; and (3) treatment therefore begins by generating a list of situations, sensations, activities, and thoughts that trigger and/or exacerbate the patient's panic and anxiety and lead to urges to escape, avoid, or employ safety behaviors to cope.

4.2.2 Assessing Panic-Related Stimuli

The next step is to generate a comprehensive list of as many of the internal and external trigger stimuli as possible (i.e., situations, activities, sensations, thoughts, images, and feelings that appear to produce the patient's panic attacks); these triggers will be used later as the basis for creating exposure exercises.

Internal Triggers: Somatic Sensations and Cognitive Symptoms
Identify any somatic (physiological) sensations and cognitive symptoms (mind going blank, difficulty concentrating, etc.) and note how much the patient fears or avoids experiencing these sensations and symptoms, what the patient does to facilitate escape and/or avoidance, and any mistaken beliefs that the patient has about them. Examples of questions to elicit this information include: What kinds of sensations make you feel anxious? What do you think it means when you have this symptom? What do you think will happen if you experience this symptom unexpectedly? Why do you try to avoid or compensate for having these sensations and symptoms? These questions could be paired with the administration of an empirically supported ROM

measure, such as the Body Sensations Questionnaire (BSQ; Chambless et al., 1984 – see Appendix 2).

External Triggers: Situations and Activities

Identify all situations, places, and activities that evoke fear, panic sensations, and/or urges to avoid and engage in safety behaviors. Include situations that the patient may enter, but only if accompanied by someone they trust. Examples may include crowded places, open spaces, bridges, tunnels, elevators, theaters, being alone at home, being far from home, playing sports. Patients may also avoid eating or drinking certain foods and beverages that impact them physiologically, such as caffeine. Examples of questions to elicit this information include: What kinds of situations make you feel anxious? What kinds of activities make you feel anxious? Is there anything you are not doing at the moment because of your panic attacks? Is there any part of your lifestyle (e.g., diet or exercise) that you have changed due to your panic attacks? These questions can be paired with the administration of an empirically supported ROM measure, such as the Mobility Inventory for Agoraphobia (Chambless et al., 1985; see Appendix 3).

4.2.3 Assessing Cognitive Features

Cognitions play a critical role in CBT approaches to panic disorder

Given the key role that cognitions play in both CBT models of panic, it is particularly important to obtain information about the cognitive biases that are playing a role in the initiation and escalation of the panic cycle, as well as the perpetuation of the patient's fears. This information can be used to aid in the development of effective exposure-based interventions, as well as cognitive interventions.

In panic disorder, both CBT models suggest that perceiving external and internal triggers cause patients to generate negative predictions that generate anxiety, which in turn leads to the amplification of somatic and cognitive symptoms. The amplification in symptoms may initially be very slight, but because patients with panic are hypervigilant for internal and external "threats," they become adept at detecting these increases and begin to feel an urgency to manage or control them as they also begin to recall unpleasant memories of previous attacks. Unfortunately for the patient, these attentional biases, negative thoughts, and efforts to control have a paradoxical effect on the anxiety, which is then "catastrophically misinterpreted" as further evidence that things are getting worse (cf. Austin & Richards, 2001; Clark, 1986). Thus, it is critical for the therapist to gather all of the negative predictions and catastrophic misinterpretations that the patient experiences during each step in the panic attack cycle and focus on predictions about the likelihood as well as their feared consequences of having a panic attack. Examples include believing that feeling dizzy is a sign that they will pass out or that a racing heart is a sign of an impending heart attack, predicting they will have a panic attack every time they enter a crowded place, predicting that if their mind goes blank or if they feel out of body or believe things are not real, it will mean that they are losing their mind or going crazy and/or will lose control and would end up on a psychiatric inpatient ward, or predicting that people will notice if they had a panic attack and label them as "weak" or "crazy." Examples of questions to elicit this information include: What kinds of anxiety-related thoughts pass through your mind when you are experiencing a panic attack? What kinds of thoughts do you try to avoid when you are out? What is the worst thing you can imagine happening if you were to have a panic attack? What do you think might happen if you unable to escape or avoid places in which you might have a panic attack or help was not available? How likely do you think it is that people can see tell when you are having a panic attack? What do you think other people would think if they saw you having a panic attack? These questions can be paired with the administration of an empirically supported ROM measure, such as the Agoraphobic Cognitions Questionnaire (ACQ; Chambless et al., 1984; see Appendix 1).

Many patients also develop a "fear of fear," predicting that their anxiety or panic attacks and the associated unpleasant and scary bodily sensations will persist indefinitely or spiral out of control if they do not do something to avoid or escape from experiencing them or neutralize them in some way. For example, patients may fear that unless they get out of the situation their anxiety will escalate until they lose control. Questions to help elicit these types of cognitions include: Do you worry that you will become anxious and the anxiety will never go away? What might happen to you if you remained anxious for long periods of time? Because this type of fear is not always readily apparent to the patient, some patients have difficulty articulating that what they fear is actually the experience of feeling very anxious, i.e., sensations associated with the panic attack or fight or flight response. These patients might require some prompting to be able to describe such concerns.

> Panic disorders and agoraphobia are often linked with a "fear of fear"

4.2.4 Assessing Behavioral Features

In addition to obtaining information about the role that negative cognitions play in the panic cycle, the therapist should also assess for problematic behavioral patterns that the patient may employ in response to their fears – while experiencing a panic attack, between panic attacks, and in order to prevent a panic attack from occurring – as such responses, while often providing short-term relief, become negatively reinforced, and ultimately serve to maintain anxiety and panic attacks in the long-term (Barlow, 2004; Barlow et al., 2004; Bögels & Mansell, 2004; Clum & Knowles, 1991; Newman & Llera, 2011). This includes actively avoiding situations outright (e.g., certain crowded places such as movie theaters or stadiums or other situations such as driving during rush hour or on busy highways) out of a fear of experiencing a panic attack, escaping from situations (i.e., leaving while anxiety is rising or high due to a fear of what will happen if they stay), and utilizing safety behaviors to manage their symptoms in situations that they cannot avoid.

There is some debate in the field as to whether all safety behaviors need to be identified and targeted for elimination in order to maximize the

Judicious use of safety behaviors may make exposure therapy more acceptable for some clients

efficacy of the treatment, with some researchers (e.g., Blakey et al., 2019; Levy & Radomsky, 2014; Rachman et al., 2008) suggesting that allowing the judicious use of safety behaviors during exposure therapy may improve treatment acceptability/tolerability without diminishing its efficacy. Either way, the therapist should certainly strive to identify all safety behaviors (see Funayama et al., 2013, for an approximate guideline on how to identify safety behaviors among patients with panic disorder, and Box 1 for a list of common safety behaviors in panic disorder) and then collaborate with the patient about how best to flexibly test out exposure – with or without them.

> **Box 1**
> **Common Safety Behaviors in Panic Disorder**
> - Checking pulse/breathing
> - Checking for the presence of bathrooms
> - Carrying safety aids, lucky charms, or other comforting objects
> - Keeping a water bottle, rescue medication, or a cell phone nearby at all times
> - Sitting near exits and/or making sure there is a clear path to escape a situation
> - Avoiding caffeinated beverages
> - Walking slowly or rigidly
> - Leaning on walls for support
> - Distracting self while traveling
> - Being accompanied by trusted person in activities
> - Seeking reassurance

Finally, the therapist should also assess for any potential cognitive processes that may be influencing the avoidant behaviors. Examples of questions to elicit this information include: What sensations or situations do you avoid because of your fears? Can you ever confront this situation? How does avoiding these situations make you feel more comfortable? What do you do when you cannot avoid such a situation? Tell me about the strategies or subtle things you do to reduce your fears of having a panic attack. How does doing these things reduce your discomfort? What might happen if you did not use these strategies?

4.2.5 Self-Monitoring

Self-monitoring is a critical part of CBT

To help further refine the functional assessment as well as aid in treatment planning and assessing the impact of the treatment program over time, ask the patient to complete the following forms between sessions: (a) a daily mood record documenting their anxiety, depression, and mood, as well as any medications they took, and overall fear of having a panic attack, and (b) a panic attack record to be completed as soon as possible after each panic attack in order to keep a real-time log of all panic attacks, as well as any triggers that led to them (see Appendix 4). Be sure to provide a rationale for having the patient complete the forms, emphasize the importance of doing so, and instructions for completing them during the initial treatment session. It is also often helpful to complete a sample entry (e.g., using a recent panic attack) that the patient can then use as a template for their homework. It may also be useful to have a plan for when they will complete the daily mood record and how they will ensure they have a copy of the panic attack record with them at all times. Finally, it may be helpful to anticipate any potential challenges and problem solve ahead of time.

Some patients fail to carefully and accurately self-monitor because they do not appreciate the task's relevance. To increase adherence, convey the following:

> Self-monitoring helps both me and you gain an accurate picture of the time spent engaged in and situations that lead to panic attacks. It helps you identify triggers for the panic attacks that you may not be aware of. Some patients use the fact that they have to report their panic attacks to the therapist as motivation to resist experiencing panic attacks. Accurate reporting of panic attacks between now and the end of treatment will reveal how much progress you have made in therapy.

Give the following instructions:

> Rather than guess, from now on let's record each panic attack you have, either as you have it or soon thereafter. To avoid forgetting the important details, please fill out all details on the panic attack record, which include where you were, how long the attack lasted, which was the first symptom, how high your anxiety got, all the other symptoms that were involved and whether you did anything to cope.

A useful way to train patients to self-monitor is to review a recent attack with the patient and have them practice recording the information on the panic attack record. To further increase adherence, tell the patient that the first item on the agenda for the next session will be to review the self-monitoring forms.

4.2.6 Psychoeducation

The psychoeducation component of CBT (e.g., Barlow & Craske, 2006; Clark & Salkovskis, 1987) helps the patient to learn about the symptoms of panic and how they are not only benign, but also *adaptive* in the presence of true danger. It also helps the patient to conceptualize the etiology and perpetuation of panic symptoms based on the cognitive behavioral model. Finally, it explains to the patient how these symptoms are weakened by the techniques used in the CBT, such as interoceptive exposure, in vivo exposure, and cognitive restructuring. Data suggest that patients find psychoeducation to be both useful and liked (Cox et al., 1994) and may precede notable decreases in panic attacks (Micco et al., 2007). The main concepts to be conveyed are: (a) panic attacks are normal and commonly experienced, (b) the symptoms of panic are not dangerous, (c) panic attacks recur due to the conditioning

Providing a coherent rationale for CBT is an important component of therapy

of fear to the initial panic attack and the subsequent development of catastrophic misinterpretations of both external (situations) and internal (bodily sensations) cues associated with the initial panic attack, as well as the avoidance of the sensations and places in which one fears they may experience those sensations. Having a coherent rationale for CBT is especially important since patients who do not see how interoceptive and in vivo exposure can ultimately produce benefit, may not be willing to engage in these challenging CBT techniques.

Begin by helping the patient understand that the link between panic symptoms and the fear they generate can be broken with practice. Convey the following points: (1) The treatment techniques are based on the idea that panic attacks involve a series of patterns of dysfunctional thoughts and reactions to the panic sensations that become a vicious cycle and require help to break. (2) Maladaptive thought patterns in panic disorder involve overestimating the danger associated with panic sensation or situations in which the patient fears the sensations will occur, which leads to feeling anxious when certain situations and thoughts and symptoms become encountered. (3) The anxious feelings lead to further body sensations, which then are misinterpreted further as signs or evidence that the worst-case scenario is beginning to happen. (4) This escalates the perception of threat in the patient, which further escalates feelings of anxiety until a full-blown panic attack is experienced. The maladaptive behavioral patterns include avoidance, escape, and various safety behaviors that the patient engages in to reduce their anxiety or anxious apprehension. (5) These avoidance, escape, or safety behaviors are counterproductive because they only reduce anxiety temporarily and prevent new learning from occurring. Yet, in doing so, they become stronger and stronger habits due to the relief one feels from the reduction of anxiety.

Cognitive and behavioral models of panic (Barlow & Craske, 2006; Clark, 1986) suggest that patients also become hypervigilant for signs of "danger" (i.e., panic) – be they external situations in which a panic attack is perceived as likely to occur, or internal sensations associated with panic. In addition, patients develop anticipatory anxiety whenever they are unable to avoid these danger signals, which only becomes stronger after longer periods of avoidance. Thus, a closed-loop system is formed in which the patient avoids situations in order to prevent an anticipated catastrophic event from happening, but this ultimately leads to higher increased anticipatory anxiety in situations the patient cannot avoid. Patients enter these situations hypervigilant for signs that a panic attack may occur and are thus more likely spot the shifts in their physiology generated by their own anticipatory anxiety, which confirms their fears of a panic attack starting. This in turn leads to greater anxiety and more intense symptoms until the thinking and behavioral patterns in panic disorder become so intense that they disrupt the patient's life.

Normalizing Panic Attacks

Infrequent panic attacks are present to some degree in all populations. In fact, in the US population, the lifetime prevalence of panic attacks has been estimated as high as 22.7% (Heuer et al., 2009). This lines up both with earlier studies suggesting that there may have been an increase in the prevalence of panic attacks among adults 25–74 years of age in the general US population between 1980 and 1995 (Goodwin, 2003), and more recent studies suggesting there may have been an increase in the prevalence of panic attacks among adults under 50 years of age (with a more rapid increase among young adults) in the US between 2008 and 2018 (Goodwin et al., 2020). The exact cause of panic attacks remains unknown. However, people who go on to develop panic disorder may do so due to a combination of biological and psychological vulnerabilities that then lead them to begin to fear experiencing these attacks again and look out for signs of future attacks going forward. Whereas people who do not go on to develop panic disorder find a way to rationalize the experience rather than develop catastrophic beliefs about it, and do not react with increased sensitivity to their somatic symptoms.

> The lifetime prevalence of panic attacks in the US is approximately 23% and is increasing

Many patients are often surprised and relieved to find out that just about anyone can experience a panic attack at some point in their life. If the patient wants to know why people have panic attacks in the first place, the therapist should explain that everyone's body occasionally has glitches. Certain people react to these random sensations with fear, anxiety, or trepidation, which then becomes conditioned to the sensations so that they then begin to associate these sensations with fear.

Underscore that the problem in panic disorder is not that the symptoms occur per se, but it is how the patient *reacts* to these symptoms. As long as a patient interprets these sensations as threatening, they are at risk for developing a panic disorder. Thus, the aim of treatment is not to eliminate panic attacks altogether but rather to correct the patient's misperception of these attacks and reduce the amount of distress that gets associated with this misperception. Once these panic sensations are no longer seen as threatening, it does not matter when or how frequently they occur.

Ask the patient to review a quality source of psychoeducational information on the causes of anxiety and panic between sessions for homework. Normalizing panic attacks is useful for patients with panic disorder, as is explaining how the physiology behind panic works and dispelling common myths. One excellent source of information that is widely available on the internet is the handout entitled *The Nature and Causes of Anxiety and Panic* (Powers et al., n.d.). This document defines anxiety and panic, explains the function of anxiety and panic, and describes common situations and sensations that patients with panic disorder report. It then presents a CBT model of panic and describes each component. Finally, it ends by listing and then dispelling some of the common myths about panic. Another excellent source is a brochure *Panic Disorder: When Fear Overwhelms* produced by the National Institute for Mental Health (2022).

The Role of Dysfunctional Interpretations in Panic Disorder

The idea that emotional responses (e.g., fear, panic attacks) and behavioral responses (e.g., escape or avoid or implement safety behaviors) are determined by one's beliefs (e.g., perception about normal sensations associated with anxiety) and not the panic attacks per se forms the theoretical basis of CBT. Patients must understand the process by which their dysfunctional beliefs and maladaptive interpretations can lead to emotional responses such as fear and panic. Strong emotions in turn exacerbate the very somatic symptoms that the patient's fear experiencing, which are then interpreted as confirmation of their catastrophic predictions (i.e., the fear-of-fear cycle). Over time, these dysfunctional beliefs may also lead to secondary emotions such as depression, shame, and embarrassment.

> **Aaron Beck's cognitive model involves core beliefs, dysfunctional assumptions, and automatic thoughts**

According to Beck's cognitive model (Beck, 1976), dysfunctional thinking may occur on three levels: (1) core beliefs, (2) dysfunctional assumptions, and (3) automatic thoughts. Automatic thoughts are thoughts that are involuntarily activated in certain situations and provoke an emotional or behavioral response. In anxiety disorders, automatic thoughts often include overestimations of risk, catastrophizing of the predicted outcome, and underestimations of one's ability to cope.

Dysfunctional assumptions consist of rigid (and often conditional and unarticulated) attitudes and "rules for living" that patients adopt that serve to influence their view of specific situations, which in turn influences how they think, feel, and act in those situations. In patients with panic disorder, these assumptions are often unrealistic and maladaptive and make them inclined to interpret specific situations and stimuli in a catastrophic manner. For example, a patient with panic disorder may believe "It's terrible to feel anxious" and live by the maxim that 'It's better to be safe than sorry." Thus, experiencing any somatic sensations when entering a crowded place may then lead them to experience panic and subsequent escape.

> **Schemas are core beliefs about self, others, and the world**

Core beliefs, or *schemas*, are deeply held beliefs about self, others, and the world. Core beliefs are generally learned early in life and are influenced by childhood experiences and seen as absolute. In patients with panic disorder, the core beliefs might be about the panic symptoms, but they can also be related to a person's self-concept, or their family, or any part of their lives. For example, a patient with panic disorder who is also a parent may be concerned about their child's impression of them and believe that having panic disorder means they are "weak" and a "bad parent."

The cognitive model of panic disorder (Clark, 1986) proposes that panic sufferers attribute benign somatic sensations to dispositional rather than situational factors, and, in addition, interpret these sensations in a catastrophic manner. Applying the cognitive model with sensations as triggers can sometimes be challenging; however, the sensations, the maladaptive beliefs, and the misinterpretations are all internal private events. Therefore, it is important to help the patient distinguish between random, benign physiological sensations that occur in everyone and their negative automatic thoughts and appraisals of these sensations that lead to panic attacks. Indeed, Salkovskis et al. (1996; cited in Austin & Richards, 2001) demonstrated that if people with panic disorder attributed their somatic arousal to understandable causes they did not panic.

The Role of Avoidance and Safety Behaviors in Panic Disorder

It is crucial for patients to understand how their avoidance of situations and sensations and use of safety behaviors contribute to the vicious cycle of panic disorder (Barlow & Craske, 2006; Clark, 1986). This can then serve as the foundation for engaging in interoceptive and in vivo exposure and elimination of safety behaviors. Discuss the following points with the patient. Review how perceiving physiological sensations as dangerous or catastrophic increases their feelings of anxiety and how escaping or avoiding or engaging in safety behaviors decreases their anxiety – temporarily/in the short term. Note that along with the outwardly observable/obvious behaviors, there are also other, more covert/subtle (and often cognitive) strategies that people with panic disorder often use that serve the same function.

Inform the patient that these strategies are collectively termed "safety behaviors" because they help people feel safe, and, in so doing, convince themselves that by utilizing these tools, they have managed to avoid experiencing some catastrophic outcome. Some patients may fear that other people would see their patterns of escape, avoidance, and safety behaviors as bizarre or odd, and therefore feel embarrassed or ashamed to disclose them. Normalize these tendencies and help the patient see how many people with panic disorder employ similar anxiety-reduction strategies. Give an example of how safety behaviors can be effective in reducing panic-related anxiety – in the short term. Be sure that the patient understands the functional relationship between the panic-related thoughts and urge to escape, avoid, or use safety behaviors.

Note that escaping, avoiding, or engaging in safety behaviors are all considered adaptive responses if there is a true danger present (e.g., a car veering toward your lane while you are driving). However, in the case of panic disorder, their fear is based on the misinterpretation of otherwise neutral or benign cues. In other words, their response is like a false alarm: inaccurate at best, and counterproductive at worst. In addition, note how when patients avoid situations due to feeling anxious and predicting that a catastrophe was imminent, they never get to learn whether their catastrophic prediction was in fact accurate. However, the relief they feel in the short term may convince them that they really must have "just missed" a catastrophe from occurring (i.e., negative reinforcement).

Give some examples of typical patterns of avoidance (ideally using examples taken from your assessment with the patient). For example, you consider going to a crowded movie theater, start to feel anxious, and then avoid going. Therefore, you don't have a panic attack and conclude it is because you did not go into the theater. Avoidance also keeps the patient from learning the feared situation was not really dangerous. When situations or sensations cannot be avoided, the next best solution is to search for ways to escape from the feared situation or reduce the feelings artificially as quickly as possible. Provide examples of escape behaviors, ideally using examples taken from your assessment with the patient. Because these escape strategies also reduce anxiety, they develop into "tools" that are added to the avoidance and safety behavior toolbox (all of which maintain anxiety via negative reinforcement). Distraction strategies are yet another maladaptive response that produces a temporary escape, but only serve to make things worse in the long run. Give examples of the patient's distracting responses.

In summary, avoidance, escape, and safety behaviors are common and helpful responses to the actual threats. However, patients with panic disorder mistakenly apply these same strategies to the benign bodily sensations commonly found in a panic attack, deeming them helpful because they reduce anxiety in the moment, even though they backfire in the long run. Treatment will attempt to weaken these patterns by creating opportunities for the patient to learn that avoidance, escape, and the use of safety behaviors are not necessary to reduce anxiety or prevent negative outcomes from occurring.

Presenting the Rationale for CBT

> **Patients who are enthusiastic about CBT are more likely to be successful than those with reservations about the approach**

An accumulating body of research suggest that clients who enthusiastically buy into a CBT rationale show more favorable outcomes (Addis & Carpenter, 2000). Therefore, once the patient has a grasp of the cognitive behavioral model, present the rationale for CBT by discussing the following points: The treatment techniques of interoceptive exposure, in vivo exposure, and cognitive restructuring are designed to weaken the maladaptive reactions to the physiological sensations in panic attacks and agoraphobic patterns of behavior that result as a way of coping with panic attacks. More specifically, interoceptive exposure involves gradually and systematically confronting the physiological sensations that evoke anxiety. In vivo exposure involves gradually and systematically confronting the situations that evoke anxiety – both accompanied and alone. Cognitive restructuring involves making clear predictions of what the patient fears will happen when confronting the sensations and situations, and then revisiting these predictions in order to check their accuracy.

In essence, exposure therapy is simple – though certainly not easy. The goal is to repeatedly confront sensations and situations that evoke anxiety in order to help the patient learn that their symptoms are not dangerous and that, in fact, anxiety does not remain elevated indefinitely and will not spiral out of control. Instead, anxiety actually subsides. This process is called habituation. Since the patient usually escapes from the feared situations before their anxiety subsides, they never have the opportunity to experience habituation and learn that it eventually occurs. Exposure therapy also helps patients learn that the fears related to their sensations do not occur, even if they do not escape. In order to explain the concept of habituation, draw graphs similar to that in Figure 5 to depict that within and between session habituation curves over the course of several exposure sessions.

Discuss the graph to emphasize the following points: The patient should expect to feel anxious at times, especially when starting to confront their feared situations or sensations. This distress is temporary and will eventually subside if the patient remains in the feared situation or in contact with the feared sensation long enough without using any safety behaviors. The graph shows what happens with repeated and prolonged exposures.

At the start of the first session, discomfort increases sharply ("the first is the worst") and then declines as time passes. At the second session, the discomfort subsides more quickly because new learning has taken place and

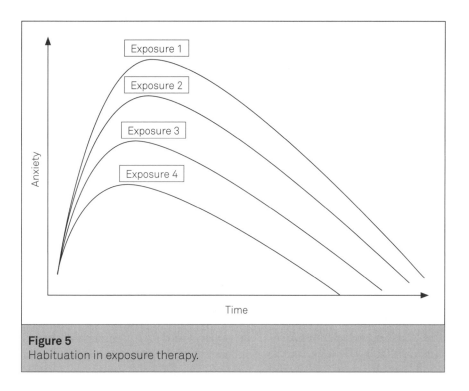

Figure 5
Habituation in exposure therapy.

previous expectancies were violated. After several exposure trials, the initial distress level is lower, and it subsides even more quickly because the patient has learned that the situation is not highly dangerous. With repeated practice, the feared situations no longer produce or provoke anxiety. This pattern only occurs if the exposure exercise is carefully designed and if the patient remains exposed for a long enough time without performing any safety-seeking behaviors.

The patient must invest in feeling anxious in order to have a less anxious future ("pain tolerance"). In most cases of panic disorder, two kinds of exposure will be necessary: (1) interoceptive exposure, which involves facing feared bodily sensations; and (2) in vivo exposure, which involves facing feared situations in real life. Exposure is the key active ingredient in CBT for panic disorder, but it must be done correctly in order to get good results.

Next, discuss how you will work with the patient and tailor the program to their needs.

Although they may share the same diagnosis, each patient with panic disorder is unique, and therefore the patient and therapist should collaborate when generating a list of items to be used in interoceptive and in vivo exposure. For interoceptive exposure, it may be helpful to use an empirically based ROM measure (e.g., the BSQ) as a starting point. In addition, although patients may report that certain sensations generate little or no anxiety, it is often useful to run through a series of exercises that generate each of the sensations associated with a panic attack, just to be certain.

Before starting these exercises, however, it is important that patients be in good health. Fortunately, many patients with a history of panic disorder have presented to emergency rooms on numerous occasions and, therefore, will have already had any potential medical issues ruled out. However, in the event that there may be some doubt as to whether the patient has any health issues that might be complicated by physical strain, they should get clearance from their primary care physician before doing interoceptive exposure exercises. While this may appear to be reinforcing panic-related fears, given that some medical conditions can be associated with panic attacks and that many patients with panic disorder have avoided exercise for years as a way of managing their fear of some of the symptoms of panic, it is important to get medical clearance before going forward. Often, the patient can bring a list of the planned interoceptive exercises (see Table 4) to their doctor to get approval to proceed.

For in vivo exposure, the Subjective Units of Distress Scale (SUDS) is still commonly used to aid in the development of fear hierarchies (McCabe, 2015). The SUDS requires patients to estimate the severity of their fear in a particular situation on a 0 (*no fear*) to 100 (*most severe fear*). It may also be helpful to use an empirically based ROM measure (e.g., the Mobility Inventory for Agoraphobia [MI]), as it includes the most commonly reported agoraphobic situations and asks patients to rate each twice – once for how much they would avoid it if facing it alone, and a second time based on how much they would avoid it if allowed to be accompanied by a trusted companion. In addition, the total score on the MI can be used to compare the patient's level of severity to other patients presenting with panic disorder with agoraphobia. Finally, if administered at various points throughout treatment (or even pre/post), the MI can be used as an objective measure of progress over time (or outcome).

Whether or not the MI is used as an aid, the feared and avoided situations are traditionally listed, rated using SUDS, and then arranged from least anxiety provoking to most anxiety provoking. Exposure exercises are then planned ahead of time, especially if they require that the therapist and patient meet in a place that has been avoided. With the rise of teletherapy, however, it is becoming increasingly easy for therapists to "accompany" patients on in vivo exposure exercises without ever having to leave their office. Either way, at the start of in vivo exposure, the therapist typically provides support and coaching during each exposure task and may even model it themselves, but by the end may remain quiet/neutral or even try to take on the voice of panic and/or leave the patient alone in the situation, in order to test the patient's skills and prevent the therapist from inadvertently becoming a safety behavior.

It is important to bear in mind that by advocating for exposure, the therapist is, in essence, instructing the patient to face their worst fears, and, in so doing, engage in an activity that seems very dangerous and/or involves doing things that most people would not ordinarily do. The patient must understand that the purpose of exposure is not to place them in realistically dangerous situations, but rather to help them better distinguish what is a realistically dangerous situation from one that they believe is dangerous, but really is not. The yardstick commonly used for this is to ask what the typical person in their community does, and how closely aligned the patient's actions are to this typical person.

Table 4
Interoceptive Exposure Exercises

Exercise	Method	Symptoms generated
Head rolling/shaking	Close eyes and spin or shake head for 30 seconds	Dizziness, nausea, blurred vision
Voluntary hyperventilation	Breathe very fast and very deep	Dizziness, dry mouth, tingling, sweaty palms, lightheadedness, numbness, visual disturbances, hot flashes
Stair climbing	Run up several flights of stairs (or on the spot) and stop suddenly	Heart racing/pounding, breathlessness, heavy legs
Straw breathing	Breathe through a thin straw or sip stir stick while closing mouth around it and holding nostrils closed	Increased urgency for air, feelings of suffocation, fears of choking, dizziness
Full body muscle tensing	Raise body up halfway during push-up on floor or against wall and hold	Muscle tension, tingling, shaking, hot flash
Head bobbing	Place head between knees and then quickly lift to upright position	Flashing and pressure in head (when down), lightheadedness, faintness, seeing spots (when raised)
Spinning	Close eyes and spin in chair (or while standing on spot) for 30 seconds	Dizziness, nausea, hot flashes
Hand staring	Stare at hand and repeat to self, "this is my hand"	Derealization, depersonalization
Light staring	Stare at bright (but not fluorescent) light and then try to read immediately after	Visual disturbances, blurred vision, difficulty concentrating
Throat clenching	Start to swallow and then stop halfway and hold	Throat tightness, fears of choking
Chest breathing	Lock hands behind head, pull elbows back, take deep breath, and then continue to take chest breaths once per second	Chest pain, restricted breathing, increased urgency for air, fears of suffocation
Increased body temperature	Wear extra sweaters and use portable office heater	Hot flashes

Sometimes in exposure therapy it is useful to push (safely) beyond what most people currently do, in order to overcorrect any irrational fears (e.g., pretend to panic in front of others to test out whether people are judgmental or cruel or, rather, can in fact be quite helpful). These tasks are designed to further weaken the panic symptoms and violate expectations in the short term and also allow room for regression in the long term (after treatment is terminated). The relationship between patient and therapist in CBT is analogous to that between a student and teacher or between an athlete and a coach.

A *mountain guide metaphor* may be helpful here: A mountain guide cannot physically push or pull their patient up the mountain. They cannot do the hard work for them. Their usefulness lies in having expertise specific to the task of mountaineering and knowledge of a particular mountain the patient wants to climb, that they can share with their patient in order to avoid common pitfalls and get to the top safely. But the patient also needs to have the right tools, the right motivation and commitment, the right preparation, and then ultimately needs to walk the trails themselves.

4.2.7 Using Cognitive Therapy Techniques

Cognitive therapy techniques for panic disorder teach patients to identify, evaluate, and modify dysfunctional thinking patterns about panic. These dysfunctional thinking patterns generate anxiety and urges to escape or avoid or utilize safety behaviors in order to prevent some catastrophic outcome from occurring. Through cognitive restructuring, patients are helped to develop more balanced and realistic beliefs about anxiety-evoking situations and sensations.

The Role of Cognitive Therapy in CBT for Panic Disorder
Research (e.g., Beck, 1988; Clark, 1986) shows that cognitive therapy alone can be effective in reducing panic attacks. However, in clinical practice, cognitive approaches are often coupled with behavioral approaches in order to maximize new learning while targeting physiological sensations and avoided situations (Micco et al., 2007; Pompoli et al., 2018; Wolf & Goldfried, 2014). This can be accomplished in a number of ways, including: (1) eliciting feared predictions before engaging in exposure and then using cognitive restructuring to correct any cognitive errors and/or distortions, (2) interweaving identifying and then either challenging or simply noticing of maladaptive beliefs and assumptions while engaging in interoceptive and in vivo exposure exercises, and (3) conducting a postmortem after an exposure exercise has been completed, asking questions such as: What did you worry would happen? Was it as bad as you expected? Did that surprise you? What would happen if we did it a little longer? What did you learn?

Using Cognitive Restructuring to Correct Cognitive Errors
Identifying in advance the ways in which the patient misinterprets sensations may be of some benefit, as it helps to raise awareness about how such thinking patterns lead to anxiety and avoidance. As was the case for interoceptive and in vivo exposure, it may be helpful to use an empirically based ROM measure (e.g., the ACQ) as a starting point. Either way, the cognitive errors can then be targeted, giving patients a cognitive tool that can then be used when engaging in the exposure exercises. Often, this is done through a combination of psychoeducation on the role that maladaptive thinking patterns play in generating and maintaining panic symptoms, along with some questions that patients can ask themselves (in the spirit of collaborative empiricism) in order to challenge the veracity of their thoughts.

The therapist can review the handouts in the session and explore with the patient how the challenging questions and identification of distortions might play a role in reducing their symptoms of panic. It is important to note, however, that while often useful, the provision of this information can be perceived (and then used) as a reassurance tool by the patient, which ultimately may backfire and undermine exposure (e.g., if the patient uses the cognitive restructuring as a distraction or believes without it they certainly would not have been able to cope). On the other hand, utilizing cognitive restructuring in advance may entice otherwise reluctant patients to engage in exposure therapy, after which the cognitive restructuring in advance may be withdrawn.

A Note on Intolerance of Uncertainty
Increasingly, intolerance of uncertainty is being viewed as a transdiagnostic psychopathological mechanism across anxiety disorders (Carleton, 2012; Carleton et al., 2012; McEvoy & Erceg-Hurn, 2016; Rosser, 2019). As such, in addition to situation- and sensation-specific fears, avoidance, escape, and safety behavior use in panic disorder may be viewed as attempts to create certainty about the patient's safety from danger. In other words, patients with anxiety disorders often report that if they cannot be 100% certain of their safety in a given situation, by default it "feels" as if there is a high risk of danger, leading them to do whatever it takes to create more certainty (rather than build up a tolerance for uncertainty by facing it). In contrast, individuals who do not suffer from an anxiety disorder often demonstrate a higher tolerance for uncertainty, assuming that these same situations are relatively safe unless they see a clear sign of danger.

To reduce panic symptoms, the patient must be willing to practice living with uncertainty. Intolerance of uncertainty underlies panic fears for events that might occur in the distant future – but which trigger panic sensations now. Patients with panic disorder often argue that they cannot risk the feared event occurring. Here you can point out that they would benefit by developing an alternative less-threatening interpretation of the experience of uncertainty.

Common Cognitive Errors in Panic
Research has shown that patients with panic disorder tend to make two common cognitive errors with respect to their panic attacks that lead them to see their attacks as threatening: (1) they overestimate the probability that something bad will happen, (2) they catastrophize the consequences of the attack, and (3) they underestimate their ability to cope. These types of predictions ultimately serve to fuel the very attacks patients fear since they imply the physical dangers involved in having a panic attack are quite likely to occur and, when they occur, they will be very bad, and they will not be able to cope. It is important to address all three of these common cognitive errors.

Cognitive techniques can help the patient develop more realistic ways of thinking about the probability, the feared consequences of a panic attack, and whether they would not be able to cope. With regard to overestimations of

> Overestimating risk, catastrophizing, and underestimating ability to cope are common cognitive errors in patients with panic disorder

probability, for example, a patient may overestimate the likelihood of having a heart attack or passing out during a panic attack (Clark, 1988). They may also predict that if they had a panic attack, they would lose control or go crazy. In addition to providing psychoeducation about the CBT model of panic and how the body works, you can encourage the patient to ask a series of questions (see Appendix 6) in order to challenge some of their notions about the likelihood of something bad happening. Examples include: (1) What percentage likelihood is it that this event will happen? (2) What evidence do I have that this is likely to happen? Do I have any evidence that it is not likely to happen? (3) How many times have I predicted this would happen? How many times has it actually happened? Remember, the goal here is not to try to prove that their fear consequences will not happen, but rather to teach them to make a rational and realistic assessment of how likely it is that something will occur.

With regard to catastrophizing, it's important to validate that idea that when people are anxious, they tend to catastrophize outcomes (Clark, 1988; Keogh & Asmundson, 2004). Explain to the patient that this simply means that we tend to exaggerate how bad we believe an outcome will be if it were to occur. Making matters worse, we also tend to lose sight of our natural ability to manage negative outcomes (i.e., resiliency), which is the third common cognitive error: the minimization of their ability to cope.

Encourage the patient to ask questions (see Appendix 6) in order to critically evaluate how bad it would actually be, and what they would actually do if their feared outcome was to happen. Examples include: (1) If it did happen, what would be the worst consequence? (2) Is it a horror or a hassle? (3) Have you experienced something like that before? What did you do to cope? (4) What could you do? How would you cope?

It is important to note that these beliefs often persist despite the fact that patients with panic disorder will have typically experienced numerous panic attacks without the feared outcomes happening. This suggests that patients likely filter away important evidence that contradicts their predictions and also that they tend to develop inaccurate theories to explain what happened. For example, a patient who has avoided using public transportation in recent months may mistakenly believe that it is only because they have taken cabs that they are still alive as, by doing so, they have not experienced a panic attack that otherwise would have killed them. In these cases, it will be important to review the Section 4.2.6 on psychoeducation explaining to the patient how avoidance, escape, and safety behaviors all serve to maintain their fears in the long term, and then emphasize the importance of engaging in exposure in order to test these beliefs.

4.2.8 Planning for Interoceptive and In Vivo Exposure

There are two main goals of interoceptive and in vivo exposure in panic disorder. The first is based on traditional models, which emphasize the role of habituation (i.e., diminishing anxiety connected to a feared but not objectively dangerous stimulus through repeated presentations). This is accomplished by focusing both on within-session habituation and between-session habituation. The second is based on inhibitory learning models (e.g., Craske et al., 2014), which place relatively less emphasis on the importance of fear habituation and belief disconfirmation and instead focus on the consolidation of new learning regarding an anticipated negative outcome and the nonoccurrence of the anticipated event.

As such, when providing the rationale for exposure, the therapist should explain that repeated and prolonged exposure frequently leads to a reduction in anxiety over time. This includes the anxiety that the patient feels during the actual exposure session, as well as the anxiety the patient feels over a series of consecutive exposure sessions. A clinical guideline that is often used to determine the length of an exposure session is to wait until the patient experiences a 50% reduction from their starting level of anxiety. Explain that if the patient can feel this reduction in anxiety – without the use of safety behaviors – and observe that their feared outcomes do not materialize, they can learn over time that their feared sensations are not as dangerous as they thought. In addition, the therapist can explain how avoidance prevents extinction learning from occurring and utilize cognitive restructuring strategies after each exposure in order to consolidate the learning that has taken place.

Building the Fear Hierarchy for Interoceptive Exposure

Interoceptive exposure is designed to create opportunities for patients with panic disorder to confront their fears about physiological sensations common to the experience of anxiety, but which are otherwise benign. However, before doing interoceptive exposure exercises it is important that a primary care physician or other medical professional rule out any potential medical conditions that are known to cause panic, as well as any health issues that might be complicated by physical strain. Often, the patient can simply bring a list of the planned interoceptive exercises (see Table 4) to their primary care physician to review and approve. Occasionally, it may be important to have the patient sign a release so that you can speak to their physician directly about the rationale for using interoceptive exposure in the treatment of panic disorder.

Once approved, the patient should be provided with a brief review of the rationale. Remind the patient that the interoceptive exposure exercises are intended to help them get used to their symptoms of panic that they have been avoiding as well as to learn something new about their symptoms and the fears they have of them. Validate the fact that it is natural to have wanted to avoid experiencing the symptoms, because avoiding them generated a sense of relief in the short term. Remind the patient that in the long term, avoidance maintained and intensified their panic disorder, as it generated more anticipatory anxiety (which intensified the very symptoms they feared, making new experiences even more challenging), and did not allow for new learning to occur. Note that in order to overcome their panic disorder, they will likely have to complete these exercises on a daily basis, over a number of weeks.

Carrying Out Interoceptive Exposure Exercises

As mentioned previously, it is often helpful to use an empirically based ROM measure (e.g., BSQ) as a starting point for assessing how frightened the patient is about the different bodily sensations associated with panic. In addition, the total score on the BSQ can be used to compare the patient's level of severity to other patients presenting with panic disorder. Finally, if administered at various points throughout treatment, the BSQ can be used as an objective measure of progress over time. However, given that some patients may self-report that certain sensations generate little or no anxiety, it is often useful to run through the entire series of interoceptive exercises together that generate each of the sensations associated with a panic attack.

The therapist should record the following information using the interoceptive exercises worksheet (see Appendix 7): (1) exposure exercise, (2) how long it was performed, (3) predicted SUDS, (4) a list of all sensations experienced, (5) the intensity (0–10) of the sensations, (6) the similarity (0–10) of the sensations to a "real" panic attack, (7) maximum SUDS (0–10), and (8) a list of all anxious thoughts experienced.

Before commencing the interoceptive exposure, the therapist should review the "rules" with the patient, which include: (1) immersing themselves into the exercise in order to experience the sensations as intensely as possible, for the full allotted time; (2) doing everything they can to not avoid experiencing the sensations, including (a) ending the exercise early, (b) distraction/not paying full attention to the sensations, and (c) use of safety behaviors. Note that while experiencing some sensation is better than nothing, patients should do their best to complete the exercise in full as this will provide you with a more accurate assessment of their fear of the sensations. You should inform the patient that in some instances the sensations will develop during the exercise, whereas in other instances the sensations will occur shortly after the exercise has ended.

Once you have worked through the entire list of exercises, you can: (a) repeat the most feared exercises in session together, (b) extend the time on each to maximize the potency of the exposure, and, perhaps most importantly, (c) assign the same exercise for the patient to do for homework between sessions. Patients may ask how often they should practice. In essence, more is better. More specifically, the patient should be encouraged to practice each assigned exercise multiple times, ideally on a daily basis, and for progressively longer periods. If it will facilitate compliance, they can certainly start with the exercises with the lowest SUDS ratings. However, ideally, they will work through them all, bottom to top if necessary, but ideally varying them and/or even combining them, on a regular basis. In addition, if not immediately, eventually they should try to complete the exercises on their own, rather than with other people around, to ensure that all cognitive safety cues are eliminated. Similarly, the patient should also try to complete the exercises in different places.

All of this should help to maximize the intensity of the exposure and create opportunities for expectancies to be violated and new learning to occur. In the spirit of inhibitory learning approaches, patients should be encouraged to only utilize cognitive restructuring strategies after each interoceptive exposure exercise has been completed, in order to consolidate the learning that has taken place. However, in the spirit of more traditional CBT models for panic disorder, patients should also be allowed to utilize cognitive restructuring strategies ahead of time, if unhelpful thoughts exist that might prevent them from completing the exercises. To aid in capturing all this information, the patient can complete an interoceptive exercises worksheet similar to the one the therapist used (see Appendix 8).

In Vivo Exposure

In the same way that interoceptive exposure was implemented to allow patients to habituate to their feared sensations, disconfirm faulty beliefs, create expectancy violations, and consolidate new learning, in vivo exposure focuses on helping patients to extend this formula to everyday activities and situations they fear and have either been avoiding or only confronting when accompanied or with the employment of safety behaviors. As mentioned previously, it is often helpful to use an empirically based ROM measure (e.g., the MI) as a starting point for assessing the degree (from 1 to 5, where 1 = *never avoid* and 5 = *always avoid*) to which the patient avoids places or situations because of their discomfort or anxiety. In addition, the total score on the MI can be used to compare the patient's level of severity to other patients presenting with panic disorder with agoraphobia. Finally, if administered at various points throughout treatment (or even pre/post), the MI can be used as an objective measure of progress over time (or outcome).

With or without the use of the MI, the goal of in vivo exposure is to collaborate with the patient to generate a list of 10–20 items, which are typically situations in which the patient expects that panic and anxiety will occur and that it would be difficult to get help in or escape from. However, it may also include activities that produce physiological arousal that patients with panic disorder and agoraphobia commonly avoid or restrict, such as exercise, drinking coffee, having sex. As was the case for bodily sensations, each situation is assigned a SUDS rating from 0 to 10, based on the predicted amount of distress that the patient expects to encounter during exposure to that particular item, using the patient's idiosyncratically derived SUDS. These items can then be sorted into a fear and avoidance hierarchy, based on their relative rankings (see Appendix 9). The fear and avoidance hierarchy then becomes the blueprint for the in vivo exposure sessions to follow. See Table 5 for an example of a fear and avoidance hierarchy.

Note that it is not essential that every possible feared or avoided situation or activity appears on the fear and avoidance hierarchy. What is important is that enough items be included to represent the full range of feared and/or avoided situations and activities, as well as the full range of the patient's SUDS – with a particular focus on the items that evoke the patient's worst fears (but are objectively not dangerous). Failure to include items that create the opportunity for the patient to confront their worst fears may ultimately reinforce their erroneous belief that such situations should be avoided because they are truly dangerous.

Table 5
Fear and Avoidance Hierarchy

Situation	Fear	Avoidance
Take plane ride on own	10	10
Exercise vigorously for 30 minutes	10	10
Drive on highway during rush hour	9.5	9
Ride in subway during rush hour	9	9
Sit in middle of aisle in crowded theater/concert	8	7.5
Stand in grocery store line during busy shopping time	7	6.5
Be at home alone	6	6
Drive on local roads, on own, during rush hour	5	4
Go for walk, on own, at least 10 blocks from home	4	3
Drink cup of coffee	3	2

In addition, it is critical that the items be described in enough detail to understand the specific fears underlying a particular item, which can then also be tested. Being detail oriented here also provides the therapist the opportunity to fine-tune items in order to capitalize on subtleties (e.g., eliminating safety behaviors) as well as break more challenging items into potentially more manageable subitems (e.g., driving on the highway during rush hour during a storm versus driving on the highway off-peak on a nice day, as opposed to just driving on a highway) and make adjustments to assignments for some of the "standard" items based on an patient's particular fears. For example, some patients with panic disorder will fear entering crowded places and therefore must eventually articulate what exactly they fear and then devise a way to confront this fear by targeting crowded places on their fear and avoidance hierarchy. Other patients with panic disorder and agoraphobia, however, will feel reassured in crowded places and instead fear being left alone or being in open and isolated spaces.

Creating a SUDS
The SUDS typically ranges from 0 (*no distress*) to 10 (*the most distress*). Occasionally patients prefer to use 0–100. Either is fine. Regardless of the range used, however, it is important to derive "anchors" based on the patient's personal experience. This way, the SUDS can be personalized in a way that has meaning to them and be anchored in personal experiences outside of their panic disorder, which they can then recall and compare to their panic-related SUDS and will not change as their panic disorder improves.

Typically, a rating of 0/10 SUDS should be connected to a time in which the patient felt no distress or discomfort at all (e.g., on a beach vacation). A rating of 10/10 SUDS should be connected to a memory (past year ideally, if not in their life) when they felt the most distress – and may have even experienced a panic attack – but which was not related to their panic disorder (e.g., experiencing intense turbulence while flying on a plane). Finally, a rating of 5/10 SUDS should be connected to a time when they felt moderate distress (e.g., taking a test, cooking for guests at a dinner party).

Once an initial list of feared or avoided items is generated and the SUDS has been created and anchored, ask the patient to assign a rating of SUDS to each item. Record the patient's SUDS rating for each item on the fear and avoidance hierarchy form (see Appendix 9). The items can then be sorted from lowest to highest. Give a copy of the fear and avoidance hierarchy form to the patient and, while collaborating with the patient, create a plan for the order in which the hierarchy items will be faced in therapy.

When designing the in vivo exposure treatment plan, the research suggests that you should: (1) begin with the item the patient predicted to be moderately distressing (e.g., 3–4/10 SUDS minimum) or above, in order to ensure that they feel anxious enough to experience habituation, as well as to generate/access their feared thoughts/predictions in order to be able to examine them afterwards; and (2) systematically work your way up to the most distressing items as efficiently as possible, ideally with several sessions left (e.g., around Sessions 6–8). This will allow new and/or previously unidentified sensations, situations, and activities to be incorporated into the hierarchy as well as maximize the time spent on the most distressing item(s), which are often require multiple exposures attempts, repeated in different contexts, to correct.

Additional guidelines for in vivo exposure include: (1) any items rated lower than the item the patient started with (e.g., less than 3–4/10 SUDS), should still be completed, but they should be done outside of the session for homework in order to facilitate generalization of skills and build a sense of self-efficacy; (2) similarly, items of the same rating as an item completed in session should be assigned for homework; and finally (3) as the treatment progresses, the patient should be encouraged to take a more active role in designing and implementing the in vivo exposure – both within the session and between sessions.

Carrying Out In Vivo Exposure Exercises

A representative item from each SUDS level, starting at moderately distressing (e.g., 3–4/10 SUDS) through to the top of their hierarchy (i.e., 10/10 SUDS) is first faced during a session (i.e., under the therapist's supervision) and assigned to be practiced for homework between sessions. Ideally, exposures should be prolonged and repeated until the item evokes little or no discomfort and/or any faulty beliefs about the nature of panic and anxiety have been corrected. Recall, however, that the most potent exposure exercises should not only focus on habituation to feared situations and the disconfirmation of faulty beliefs, but also take into account inhibitory learning approaches, and, in so doing, incorporate a blend of the eight strategies suggested for enhancing inhibitory learning (e.g., expectancy violation, deepened extinction, reinforced extinction, variability, remove safety behaviors, attentional focus, affect labeling, and mental reinstatement/retrieval cues) into the in vivo exposure exercises in order to optimize exposure.

In addition to obtaining SUDS levels before and after each exposure, the therapist may choose to encourage the patient to create certain detailed expectancies, along with ratings (0-100%) of how confident they are of the expectancies, which can be tested and reviewed and then consolidated into new learning after the exposure exercise has been completed. For example, before an in vivo exposure a patient may be most worried that, "If I have a panic attack while driving my car, I will be so incapacitated that I will have an accident." They may then rate their confidence in this happening as 90%. After the in vivo exposure exercise has been completed, the patient can then be asked whether what they were most worried about occurred and what they learned (e.g., "Feeling short of breath and experiencing a racing heart makes me nervous but doesn't necessarily mean I will have a heart attack."). See Appendix 10 for a sample in vivo exposure practice worksheet handout.

Agreeing on the Treatment Plan

Research suggests that homework compliance predicts improvement from CBT for anxiety disorders (LeBeau et al., 2013). As a result, it is crucial for the therapist and patient to agree on the rationale, importance, and plan for the exposure components of the treatment plan. Failure to do so at the beginning of treatment may ultimately result in lower treatment engagement, a lack of progress and/or generalization in the skills, and potentially even lead the patient to drop out.

Therefore, the therapist should review the following points (consider making into a treatment "contract") before starting the exposure phase of the treatment: (1) Beginning with the next session, the patient will be encouraged to practice facing their feared or avoided sensations, situations, and activities, as noted on the BSQ and as were generated during the in vivo exposure hierarchy construction. (2) Interoceptive and in vivo exposure exercises will also be assigned for homework between sessions, where they may initially be practiced under the guidance of a designated "coach," but ultimately should be practiced alone. (3) The patient should expect to feel an increase in their anxiety when first facing their feared or avoided sensations, situations, and activities. This is normal after a lengthy period of avoidance and, in fact, a good sign that patterns of avoidance are being undone. (4) The therapist will happily provide the rationale for doing exposure and initially guide the patient through each exercise, but the therapist will not provide reassurance (as this can become a safety behavior) and the patient should strive to eliminate reassurance seeking between sessions from others in their lives. (5) The patient will never be forced to complete an exposure exercise. The entire process should be collaborative and based on the rationale previously provided to the patient. The therapist will strongly encourage the patient to engage in the exposure exercises and will likely role model how to do them initially – with the idea that the patient should ultimately be motivated and committed enough to the plan to implement it on their own (without the therapist present), and without employing any safety behaviors. (6) When practiced regularly and fully, the exercises start to feel increasingly easier to complete, even if the anxiety is never completely eliminated.

Implementing Exposure: Providing the Rationale to the Patient

Although simple in concept, exposure is definitely not easy. In essence, you are asking the patient to face their deepest fears, while taking away all the "tools" they have come to rely on to get by – ideally as quickly as possible. While seasoned therapists have likely witnessed firsthand the power of this treatment for panic disorder and be tempted to dive in "guns blazing," it is important to maintain empathy for the patient and remind yourself that this is a big ask. In fact, if not presented delicately and sensitively and with a detailed explanation of the theory and rationale, it will likely result in lower treatment engagement, poor homework compliance, and potentially early dropout or outright rejection of the treatment. It is also fair to assume that motivation and commitment vary over time, so, even if highly motivated at the start of the treatment, it would be normal (and perhaps even expected) that at certain times, patients may feel less motivated and committed (especially if anxious) and need a brief refresher of the rationale.

Remind the patient that it is well established that anxiety disorders are maintained through avoidance and the use of safety behaviors. As people who experience panic attacks sincerely believe that something terrible is going to happen during an attack and experience real symptoms in their bodies (which they view as proof of their feared predictions), they often avoid particular situations or activities that bring on panic-like symptoms or make alterations in what they do in order to keep themselves "safe" when entering these situations or engaging in these activities (e.g., bring someone trusted along with them, avoid "pushing it" when exercising, carry a bottle of water everywhere).

Inform the patient that while they may believe that avoidance and the use of safety behaviors may have kept them "safe" in the short term, in the long term it has only become more distressing and is interfering with their ability to function in life. Explain that through interoceptive and in vivo exposure to these sensations and activities, they may feel more anxious in the short term as they block avoidance and finally confront their fears, but it is the only way that they can learn anything new about the true nature of their anxiety and panic and have any hope of breaking the cycle. In other words, exposure gives them the chance to gradually get used to the physical sensations, while disconfirming their fears, and testing their expectations. While the use of standard examples (or the "hip-pocket patient" strategy – see Vitousek et al., 1998) may be adequate, it is often of even greater benefit to use specific examples from the patient's history.

Explain to the patient that by continually being willing to engage in interoceptive and in vivo exposure, using a planned, gradual, and systematic method, both within sessions together and between sessions, they will become used to the physical sensations of panic and therefore less frightened by them – even if they do not fully go away or do not always behave themselves. And the beauty of exposure is that once they feel less frightened by the same symptoms that have historically held them prisoner, their confidence will increase – and so too will their motivation and commitment to go after the panic. And, thus, the panic cycle will start to be dismantled. It might not feel like it at first, but it is bound to happen – if they follow the rules of CBT. Remember, in panic disorder, they have been experiencing an exaggerated anxious response to certain internal and external cues and have done everything they can to avoid them. However, in so doing, they are out of practice in terms of facing those cues and they have never had a chance to test out whether that feared outcome actually occurs.

Note to the patient that by confronting scary but otherwise safe internal and external cues in a prolonged and repeated manner, their body adjusts and therefore begins to respond to the cues with less and less anxiety over time and, eventually, the cues lose their power to generate problematic levels of anxiety. Add that exposure exercises also allow them to develop their scientific skills – by clarifying what they are most worried will happen in certain situations, then examining whether their feared prediction actually occurred, and finally determining what they can learn from the experience.

Components of the Interoceptive and In Vivo Exposure Sessions

Assuming that sessions will be 50 minutes in order to fit with most clinical practices, the following structure for the exposure sessions is often used:
1. Mood/symptom check: 5 minutes
2. Homework check: 10 minutes
3. Interoceptive exposure exercise: 5 minutes
4. In vivo exposure exercise: 15 minutes
5. Process/discuss what was learned: 5 minutes
6. Collaborate and agree on new homework: 5 minutes
7. Select and plan next session's exposure: 3 minutes
8. Solicit feedback from the patient: 2 minutes

For the mood/symptom check, the therapist may choose to use one or more empirically supported ROM measures for panic disorder (e.g., ACQ, BSQ, MI) and/or get subjective ratings on panic severity (high, low, average out of 10) since the last session. If any comorbid conditions are present, be sure to assess these as well. If the patient is taking medications, also check on compliance.

For the homework check, the therapist should review all forms assigned and discuss the patient's effort in doing the homework. Following up on homework reinforces the message you have presented about the importance of practicing the skills between sessions. It also helps you to determine whether all instructions have been followed correctly. If the homework was not completed, the time for the homework review should be used to problem solve with the patient. If necessary, the homework from the previous week should be completed during the session before moving on. If a continual problem, it is important to assess the patient's current level of motivation and commitment; if necessary, pause the exposure therapy and implement motivation enhancement techniques. If the patient still seems unmotivated to complete the homework after attempting motivation enhancement techniques, it may be wise to discontinue the treatment – so that the patient does not mistakenly believe they received CBT and it "did not work" for their panic disorder.

When conducting the interoceptive and in vivo exposure exercises and processing what was learned, the therapist should be aware that the patient will likely be anxious and therefore be inclined to avoid or delay doing the exercises. As such, it is important to quickly introduce the exercises, starting with interoceptive exposure. Describe the specifics of the exercise, including a Socratic discussion on which symptoms the patient might expect to experience and obtain an initial rating of their SUDS. Collaborate with the patient on how long they will do the exercise, whether the therapist should role-model it (depending on where you are in treatment), what they are most worried will happen and how likely it seems, and what kinds of safety behaviors they may be tempted to employ. The therapist should record all of this on the in vivo exposure practice worksheet (see Appendix 10), which is used to track the progress over time.

Sample Script of Introduction to Interoceptive Exposure

> Therapist:
>
> At the end of our last meeting, we agreed that the interoceptive exposure task today would be for you to practice experiencing shortness of breath. Since this is your first time attempting this exercise, I will join you in this exercise. In a moment, we'll begin by voluntarily hyperventilating. To do this, you and I will speed up our breathing and shorten our breaths into short bursts. While we're doing this, I would like you to watch me, and try to mimic my pace and style of breathing. If I wave my hand at you, it means to speed up to match my pace. I also want you to intentionally focus on any catastrophic thoughts that come to mind without trying to distract yourself from them, seek reassurance from me, or use any other safety behaviors to make you less anxious. Just let the thoughts hang out in your mind and try to observe them in a detached manner.
>
> If the idea of doing this makes you feel anxious, then good! We know we are heading in the right direction, as at this point in our treatment, if you're not feeling anxious, we are not doing the right exercise! This is the only way you can find out if the bodily sensations you feel when experiencing a panic attack are dangerous and whether what you were most worried about happening actually occurred. Speaking of that, what are you most worried about happening? On a scale of 0–100, how confident are you in that belief? In addition, if you discover that your anxiety diminishes without you having to avoid or fight the sensations, it will help you gain a sense of mastery of your fear and build up your confidence for the next time you experience that symptom – and hopefully other ones too! How would you feel if you were able to learn this about your panic? What sense of accomplishment and mastery would it give you? What is your SUDS level right now, before starting this exercise? What sensations do you expect to experience? I will be keeping track of your data from this experiment on this sheet. Are you ready?

The therapist then guides the patient through voluntary hyperventilation. Immediately afterwards, the therapist instructs the patient to observe any lingering sensations while answering these follow-up questions:

> Therapist:
>
> What sensations did you experience? Tell me them all, no matter how intense they were, so I can record them all on this sheet. How intense (0–10) did the sensations get? What was your maximum distress caused by the sensations? How similar were the sensations to a "real" panic attack? Tell me all the anxious thoughts you experienced. Did what you worried about before we started this exercise occur? How do you know? What did you learn? How intense are the sensations now? What is your SUDS level now? Great, ready to do again? Can you think of anything we can do to make it more challenging this time? How would you feel if you were to try it on your own or with me outside the room? What anxious thoughts might you have about doing it this way? How confident are you in those beliefs? Should we try?

The therapist then repeats the exercise, gathering new data each time, for the duration of the time allocated to interoceptive exposure. The therapist then uses the entries on the form to search for signs that the prolonged and repeated exposure exercises are resulting in habituation of the patient's anxiety (measured via decreasing SUDS ratings) and/or that new learning is occurring (measure by decreasing ratings of confidence in the outcome(s) they are most worried about happening occurring and/or more rational beliefs being stated) – both within and between sessions. In the spirit of flexibility within fidelity (Kendall et al., 2008), there may be occasions when the therapist decides it more prudent to prioritize interoceptive exposure over in vivo exposure (and vice versa). The point is to ensure that at least a portion of each of these sessions is used for some form of exposure.

Regardless of which exposure exercises are completed in session, it is important to leave enough time for the therapist and patient to collaborate and agree on the new homework assignment. This would include which exercises will be performed, how often (ideally daily) and for how long each time (ideally at least as long as was spent in session), and how best to record the data, so they can be brought in the following week and reviewed. The patient should be reminded of the essential role that homework plays in treatment.

The therapist should also be sure that there is enough time left to select and plan the next session's exposure, especially if it will require any special tools. In addition, it is often useful for the therapist to review the patient's progress in treatment and discuss the implications of their progress on the length of treatment. Discussions and planning of this nature demonstrate your focus on helping the patient as efficiently as possible as well as your belief that their treatment can come to a successful end someday. Noting gains made helps to reinforce their motivation and commitment to the therapy. Planning together helps to keep the collaborative nature of the treatment present.

Finally, it is important to leave a couple of minutes to solicit feedback – on the treatment and your approach with them. Exposures can be challenging and, in the heat of the moment, therapist's intentions and feedback can be misheard or misunderstood. Encouraging the patient to share feedback with you allows you to address any concerns they may have and correct any misunderstandings or misconceptions about what happened or what is coming up and builds an openness and trust in the therapeutic relationship.

Conducting Exposure to the Most Distressing Stimuli

Exposure to the most feared hierarchy items should be conducted during the middle third of the treatment program. This ensures ample therapy time to sort out any unforeseen obstacles that arise while progressing up the hierarchy or that surface when attempting to confront the most difficult stimuli. Setting a clear timetable for when these exposures will take place also helps the patient understand the importance of carrying out these tasks on schedule.

> The most feared hierarchy items should be presented during the middle third of therapy

Moving Up the Hierarchy

As mentioned previously, ideally the therapist and patient should systematically work their way up to the most distressing items as efficiently as possible, so that ideally there are several sessions left to focus on the most distressing items, which often require multiple exposure attempts, repeated in different contexts, to correct. This also facilitates new learning across contexts, which in turn serves to maximize the durability of the gains made and, as such, helps decrease the odds of a relapse occurring.

Encouraging Self-Mastery

As the therapist and patient work their way down the list of interoceptive exposure items and up the exposure hierarchy, the therapist should move from leading or joining the patient in an exercise to observing and then ideally even leaving them alone or being the voice of panic during an exercise. Similarly, the therapist should deliberately move from a directive to collaborative to deferent stance to empower the patient to increasingly take charge of their therapy – both within the session and between the sessions.

The therapist may also move from structured assignments to encouraging the patient to seek out "naturalistic" (i.e., spontaneous) opportunities to face triggers, engage in interoceptive and/or in vivo exposure, eliminate safety behaviors, or test out their beliefs. Finally, the therapist engages the patient in a reverse role play in which the patient becomes the therapist and tries to help the therapist (playing a patient) understand their panic attacks, design an exposure, eliminate a safety behavior, etc. In a sense by incorporating all of this into the treatment, you are empowering patients to become their own CBT therapist.

Inform the patient that, in essence, every choice they make regarding their panic disorder will serve to either increase or decrease its power over them over time. When they choose the more challenging path of confronting their panic-related cues, they are winning – even if it does not feel like it in the moment – because they are breaking patterns of behavior and giving themselves the opportunity to learn something new. When they choose to avoid a sensation or situation or employ safety behaviors to prevent a feared catastrophe from occurring, they may feel relief in the short term, but they have just ensured more time living with panic disorder in the long term.

4.2.9 The Power of Praise – and the Risks of Reassurance

It is important to remember that patients with panic disorder typically present with tremendous distress and fear about their panic attacks. CBT can be a very challenging treatment to "sell" as it requires patients to ultimately face their biggest fears, without being allowed to do the things they normally would do to feel better.

As such, therapists need to be sensitive to the patient's experience, while also adhering to the components of treatment that have been tied to its effectiveness. More specifically, therapists must thread the needle between offering appropriate psychoeducation, encouragement, support, and praise throughout the treatment (especially during exposure exercises), while also being careful to not provide excessive reassurance, distraction, or other more subtle signs that give patients cognitive safety cues that interfere with building a tolerance for anxiety. Therapists can say things like, "You're doing a great job facing your fears – keep it up!" and "Remember, feeling anxious means you're confronting your feared triggers." Therapists are cautioned against saying things like, "Remember, you are safe. Nothing bad is going to happen." and "Keep it up and your anxiety will go down. I promise you it will get easier next time!"

4.2.10 Humor: Helpful or Hurtful?

Humor, if judiciously used, can facilitate therapy

Although little systematic empirical research conclusively supports the contention that humor in psychotherapy is beneficial (Saper, 1987), there has been a great deal of speculation since the 1970s about its therapeutic potential. This includes its properties as a tool of cognitive therapy (Gelkopf & Kreitler, 1996) and its effectiveness as a behavioral tool via the use of humorous hierarchy scenes (without relaxation) in the systematic desensitization for fear of spiders in students (Ventis et al., 2001). However, studies investigating the effects of humor trainings in clinical samples are still rare (Tagalidou et al., 2019), so caution should be used if considering its use in the treatment of patients with psychological disorders. On the one hand, it may facilitate the disentangling and distancing of the symptoms of panic, so they may be observed more mindfully. On the other hand, it may be used as safety behavior. In the worst case, it might be experienced as invalidating and cause a rupture to the therapeutic alliance.

4.2.11 Exposure for the Therapist

While the majority of mental health providers who are educated and trained in evidence-based psychological interventions would likely be able to name CBT in general, and exposure therapy in particular, as first-line interventions for panic disorder and, if quizzed, could probably describe the essence of what the treatments call on the therapist to do, ironically many therapists appear to be quite anxious about leaving the confines of their office to employ in vivo exposure with their patients. This is a shame because unless therapist concerns about exposure therapy are addressed, exposure therapy is less likely to be adopted and implemented as intended, potentially limiting its efficacy and effectiveness.

To do exposure therapy for panic disorder, you must also be willing, as a therapist, to expose yourself along the way. In the case of panic disorder, this will call on you to be willing to provoke intense physiological sensations (in yourself and your patient), as well as conduct in vivo exposure exercises as they were intended – *in vivo* – which will often mean outside of your office. This can become complicated if the therapist has a busy schedule, must travel some distance to get to an exposure situation, or is limited by their place of employment as to what they do outside of the office.

Fortunately, with the rise of secure telehealth services, the therapist can often be present and observe/coach/challenge, without having to leave their office. Should this option not be possible, then often a trusted companion or loved one is enlisted as a coach to accompany the patient on these exposure assignments. Obviously, if going out in public together for an in vivo exposure exercise, the therapist and the patient should plan in advance how the exercise will be carried out, including how to gather data to complete the in vivo exposure practice worksheet, as well as what to do in the unlikely event that either someone known to either party approaches them or the patient experiences a panic attack, etc.

Relapse Prevention
Relapse prevention is a key component found in all CBT treatments. It includes several key components that the therapist should address toward the end of therapy, including the completion and review of any evidence-based ROM measures (e.g., ACQ, BSQ, MI, Panic Disorder Severity Scale – Self Report [PDSS-SR]) that were administered at the start (and/or throughout) the treatment, a review of the CBT model of panic, a review of the rationale for treatment, a review of skills that were learned and plan on how to keep them sharp, psychoeducation on the difference between a lapse and a relapse, strategies for preventing relapses, final feedback on the work the two of you did together, and discussion of the remaining challenges in the weeks ahead.

4.2.12 Booster Sessions

For some patients, planning a brief series of booster sessions can be helpful before officially terminating treatment (Gearing et al., 2013; Whisman, 1990). This often incentivizes patients to continue to practice their skills on their own, in the real world, knowing they will be reporting back to their therapist at some point. It also allows for a gentler tapering off of treatment and termination of the therapeutic relationship for patients who may have presented with more intense symptoms and/or whose panic symptoms were significant enough at the end to warrant extending the therapy.

If choosing to utilize booster sessions, the agenda and structure of each should remain the same, with the only change being that the length of time between visits is systematically lengthened (e.g., agreeing to three booster sessions, with Booster #1 coming 1 month after the last session, Booster #2 coming 2 months after Booster #1, and Booster #3 coming 3 months after Booster #2) in order to increase the patient's sense of self-confidence and self-efficacy, and ease the transition out of therapy. In fact, each of the boosters can be considered tentative and cancelled or extended, based on how the patient is feeling closer to the time of their appointment.

Patients wanting treatment beyond the three boosters should either "recontract" (i.e., create new goals) for another round of CBT or can be referred to a trusted colleague to engage in a different format of psychotherapy that might be a better match for what they are now seeking. In addition, the therapist can provide resources such as self-help books, mobile apps, or online/in-person support groups to aid the patient after treatment has terminated.

4.3 Mechanisms of Action

From a CBT perspective, the key mechanism of action in the treatment of anxiety disorders in general, and, more specifically, panic disorder and agoraphobia, is *exposure* (i.e., the repeated approach toward fear-provoking stimuli). Exposure therapy may be administered in a variety of forms, including graduated versus intense (or flooding therapy), brief versus prolonged, with and without various cognitive and somatic coping, and imaginal, interoceptive, or in vivo (Craske et al., 2014).

Interestingly, while our understanding of mechanisms responsible for the effects of exposure therapy has traditionally focused on habituation-based models that emphasize a reduction in fear throughout exposure and behavioral testing to explicitly disconfirm threat-laden beliefs and assumptions (e.g., Foa & Kozak, 1986; Foa & McNally, 1996; Salkovskis et al., 2007), research over the past 10–15 years has given rise to inhibitory learning-based models of extinction as the central mechanism in successful exposure therapy for fear and anxiety (see Craske et al., 2008; Craske et al., 2012; Craske et al., 2014), and these inhibitory learning models have in turn led to a new set of therapeutic interventions that are often inconsistent with habituation-based models. For example, not only do the strategies derived from inhibitory learning not emphasize fear reduction per se during exposure trials, but instead may, at times, use strategies designed to maintain elevated fear throughout exposure trials (Craske et al., 2014).

Finally, further complicating the matter is the fact that inhibitory learning models overlap with cognitive models to some degree in that they both emphasize behavioral experiments to disconfirm beliefs and assumptions (Craske et al., 2014). However, inhibitory learning models are not restricted to behavioral testing as a strategy for generating inhibitory associations, nor are they limited to testing explicitly stated cognitions. Given that the two models have some elements in common, that both have been linked to extinction, and that both have demonstrated empirical support, in clinical practice many clinicians strive to weave strategies and interventions based on both models into the treatment.

4.4 Efficacy and Prognosis

Decades of research, based both on uncontrolled and randomized controlled trials evaluating the efficacy and effectiveness of CBT for patients with panic disorder and agoraphobia, have consistently shown that patients receiving this treatment make clinically significant gains by the time treatment ends, and a sizable portion maintain their gains in the weeks, months, and years following treatment. For example, one review (Margraf et al., 1993) found that approximately 80% or more of the patients receiving CBT achieved panic-free status as well as strong and clinically significant improvement in general anxiety, panic-related cognitions, depression, and phobic avoidance – and that these gains were maintained at follow-ups of up to 2 years.

In addition, CBT has been found to have a relatively rapid onset of action (Penava et al., 1998) and to be of benefit to patients who have not responded to medications (Pollack et al., 1994). For example, in a meta-analysis of 43 controlled studies for panic disorder, Gould et al. (1995) found that cognitive-behavioral treatments yielded the highest mean effect sizes (ES = 0.68) relative to pharmacological (ES = 0.47) and combination treatments (ES = 0.56). In addition, the proportion of subjects who dropped out of cognitive-behavioral treatments was 5.6% relative to 19.8% in pharmacological treatments and 22.0% in combined treatments.

Cognitive-behavioral treatments have higher effect sizes, lower dropout rates, and less "slippage" than either pharmacology or combined treatments

Finally, perhaps most impressive is that the CBT treatment showed virtually no "slippage" in effect size (–0.07) by 1-year follow-up as compared to sizable slippage (–0.46) for pharmacological treatment (Butler et al., 2006). In another meta-analysis, Oei et al. (1999) compared panic patients' scores at the end of treatment and at follow-up against community norms and found that CBT reduced symptoms to levels near or below those found in the general population by end of treatment and these treatment gains were maintained over an unspecified follow-up interval (Butler et al., 2006).

4.5 Variations and Combinations of Methods

4.5.1 Variants of CBT Treatment Procedures

CBT for panic disorder has been studied extensively, including as a complete package, when using "active ingredients" that have been isolated and then administered alone or in some combination, and when combined with medications. In addition, numerous alternatives to the traditional individual, in-person, face-to-face format, have been studied, including CBT for panic disorder administered by telephone, in a digital-assisted modality, to groups of people, and when using guided or unguided self-help therapy in which patients work through a standardized protocol independently that can, in turn, be in book format or delivered via the internet. For an extensive review, see Papola et al., (2020).

4.5.2 CBT and Medications

> Both CBT and SSRIs are first-line treatments for panic disorder and agoraphobia

Most expert consensus statements and treatment guidelines consider both CBT and SSRIs as first-line treatment interventions for panic disorder and agoraphobia. As such, many mental health providers then conclude that combining CBT with medications would therefore be synergistic and lead to outcomes greater than either treatment delivered on its alone. Yet, despite the decades of research that has gone into examining CBT and medications for panic disorder (as well as CBT *versus* medications for panic disorder), there is surprisingly little well-designed research examining the impact of delivering CBT and medications alone versus in combination.

Foa et al. (2002) conducted a comprehensive literature search of published randomized trials that compared combined treatment with medications or CBT as monotherapies across all the anxiety disorders and found a total of only 10 studies that met their inclusion criteria (and only three studies met their inclusion criteria for panic disorder). With such a small sample size then, it is near impossible to draw any meaningful, empirically based conclusions. With this caveat in mind, Foa et al. (2002) noted that only one of three studies (Barlow et al., 2000) they included for panic disorder found an advantage for combined treatment over CBT alone at posttreatment, whereas another one of the three studies they included (Marks et al., 1993) found combined treatment superior only to medication.

Foa et al. (2002) suggested that the more interesting findings emerged at follow-up, where two of the three studies they included found that combined treatment interfered with long-term maintenance of gains of CBT, which they hypothesize was due to the fact that, ironically: (a) in diminishing anxiety responses, medications may hamper the ability of CBT exercises to disconfirm the erroneous beliefs associated with these responses; and (b) the absence of disasters is then attributed to the medication rather than to the distorted beliefs. This finding makes sense if viewed through the lens of the CBT models of panic disorder described in this volume and is consistent with other studies such as Otto et al. (1993) who found that medication that suppresses panic impedes the necessary cognitive changes for long-term maintenance of gains in panic disorder, and Başoglu et al. (1994) who found that patients who at the end of 8 weeks of treatment attributed their gains to medication were more likely to relapse than those patients who attributed their gains to their own efforts. Given the above findings, a strategy that has often been adopted is to offer the treatments sequentially, rather than simultaneously, and to only utilize the additional treatment if the first treatment was not as successful as hoped. It is also important to note that other factors, such as cost, access, comorbidity, preference, should also play a role in determining which is initially selected.

4.6 Problems in Carrying out the Treatment

Box 2 lists common problems that arise in carrying out CBT for panic disorder and agoraphobia. Suggestions for managing each obstacle are provided in Sections 4.6.1 to 4.6.9.

Box 2
Common Obstacles in Carrying out CBT for Panic Disorder and Agoraphobia

- Organization of suitable treatment settings or preconditions
- Negative reactions to psychological interventions and the CBT model
- Resistance and other issues with patient motivation and commitment
- Therapist's discomfort when conducting exposure exercises
- Therapist's need to provide certainty
- Problems in the patient–therapist working alliance
- Cognitive therapy techniques and somatic skills that become safety behaviors
- Unbearable anxiety levels during exposure
- Absence of anxiety during exposure

4.6.1 Organization of Suitable Treatment Settings or Preconditions

Ironically, one of the biggest challenges in treating panic disorder – particularly if accompanied by agoraphobia – is the patient's ability to get to the clinic. Patients often report that their panic disorder and agoraphobia are so severe that they cannot make it in for treatment. Traditionally, therapists had several options for managing this obstacle, including allowing the person to be accompanied to the office by a trusted companion, offering phone coaching, and offering the option of home visits. More recently, with advances in technology, many therapists now also offer the option of video sessions using a video conferencing tool compliant with the Health Insurance Portability and Accountability (HIPAA) Act.

Hospital administrators and insurance companies may have trouble conceptualizing the need for off-site, in vivo treatment of patients

Another setting challenge that many therapists continue to face is being able to conduct in vivo exposure with their patients, as many large institutions, unfamiliar with this evidence-based component of CBT for panic disorder and other anxiety disorders, have policies around safety, legal, and compliance that restrict provider activities/interactions with patients outside of the office. To address these institutional hesitations, providers can cite the vast empirical literature supporting in vivo exposure as a gold-standard, first-line treatment for panic disorder, note the thousands of studies that have been completed using in vivo exposure without incidence, and offer to modify the consent form to include a clause that addresses this component of the treatment.

Finally, even therapists who are permitted to do in vivo exposure outside of the office must have the time and flexibility in their schedule to be able to travel to and from the patient's feared situations, as well as to conduct the actual in vivo exposure component of the session. Again, with the rise of teletherapy as a viable and increasingly accepted option, most of these traditional obstacles can be overcome.

4.6.2 Negative Reactions to Psychological Interventions and the CBT Model

Recall that patients with panic disorder often first present to their primary care physician due to the intensity of the somatic sensations they experienced. Given that the physical sensations are real and not "in their head," some patients have a difficult time accepting that they in fact do not have a medical problem but rather have a psychological disorder. As such, they often either seek a medical intervention, or, if that is ruled out, a medication, as medications at least appear to be acceptable as an intervention, given they are more easily connected to the patient's beliefs about the medical nature of their problems and/or the "chemical imbalance" that they assume must be responsible for their panic symptoms.

As a result, these patients often believe that psychotherapy in general, and CBT in particular, will not be helpful. In fact, with its emphasis on the primary role that cognitions play in the generation and perpetuation of panic, offering a course of CBT is often misinterpreted by patients to mean the therapist is suggesting that their panic is "all in their head" – leading them to either reject the treatment outright or drop out before completing a full course of treatment. In order to overcome this obstacle, therapists can offer psychoeducational materials on the nature of panic and anxiety, present the CBT model interactively using one of the patient's recent panic attacks as an example to see whether or not it "fits" with the model, and emphasize that the CBT model of panic focuses more on perpetuating factors then etiological factors (what matters more is to address what might be maintaining the panic, as opposed to what caused it). Finally, the therapist might challenge the patient to become a "scientist" and test out whether psychological interventions can in fact play a role in helping reduce their panic attacks before ruling them out.

4.6.3 Resistance and Other Issues With Patient Motivation and Commitment

Resistance is typically defined as anything the patient does to impede the progress of psychotherapy. Although traditionally emphasized to a much greater extent in psychoanalytic psychotherapy, some forms of resistance are common to all forms of psychotherapy. In his classic text on the topic, Leahy (2001) views resistance in CBT as patients' attempts to avoid risk of further pain and suffering. Westra (2004), on the other hand, connects resistance to feelings of ambivalence about change or, by proxy, about engaging in the change-based treatment techniques found in CBT. Either way, it fits that patients with panic disorder and other anxiety disorders would instinctively employ resistance as a coping strategy at various points throughout the course of treatment, especially when being asked to make changes that could lead to short-term pain and suffering.

More specifically, the therapist should be on the lookout for resistance to: (1) decreasing and ultimately eliminating the use of avoidance as a coping strategy, while (2) following through with exposure exercises, and (3) reducing and ultimately eliminating safety behaviors while completing exposure and naturalistically when facing unplanned fear-inducing situations or sensations. To overcome these obstacles, therapists should invest time early on anticipating and normalizing these forms of resistance with the patient, and then offering strong psychoeducation on how eliminating avoidance and safety behaviors while increasing exposure to sensations, activities, and situations work together to rapidly reduce, if not eliminate, panic attacks.

The therapist can make this conversation interactive, first asking what the patient has tried to do to cope/manage and then asking them to rate how effective they think each of the tools they have used has been. The therapist can use a decisional balance (e.g., Miller & Rose, 2015) to address feelings of ambivalence about change, weighing out the pros and cons for continuing to do things in the same way versus making a change, and trying something new. Finally, if the resistance is related to high levels of anxiety, which could lead to drop out, refining the exposure hierarchy to include more intermediate items might be appropriate, if they are more acceptable and less threatening, to help the patient to engage in treatment in the short term, and eventually lead to the more challenging items.

4.6.4 Therapist's Discomfort When Conducting Exposure Exercises

One of the biggest obstacles for therapists (particularly those new to CBT) is in being comfortable implementing exposure exercises into the course of treatment. Therapists often express discomfort about the level of activity required on their part, as well as the logistics, ethics, and legalities of conducting therapy outside of their office, and the general idea of purposely encouraging a patient to confront triggers that evoke such obvious emotional discomfort.

Recall, however, that the key aspect of CBT is that the therapist and patient collaborate as scientists and work equally hard in coming up with a model of the patient's panic, and then coming up with hypotheses on how to disrupt the panic cycle, not just in the office, but outside of it. Thus, CBT in fact does call on the therapist to do extra work, in treatment planning and execution, in educating and challenging, in guiding and supporting, all in service of efficiency. In addition, while creating opportunities for patients to experience their anxiety may appear cruel, they are already experiencing it enough to be diagnosed with a disorder and being alongside them as they confront it in the short term gives them the best chance to learn something new about their feared triggers and develop new skills that will help them feel more confident to manage it on their own in the long term.

4.6.5 Therapist's Need to Provide Certainty

Many therapists feel compelled to provide certainty. This may be because: (a) they feel responsible to provide a sense of certainty about the treatment as the "expert" in the room, (b) they want to reassure the patient that their panic symptoms and/or feared situations are not dangerous, and/or (c) they mistakenly believe that the implicit goal of the cognitive interventions in CBT is to create certainty that negative thoughts are "wrong." While all seem reasonable in their intent, each of these strategies that the therapist is inclined to use to provide certainty is not only problematic for the treatment, but also inherently flawed – as there is no way to create absolute certainty – about whether the treatment will help (and if so, how much) a particular patient, about the symptoms not being a sign of something dangerous (not likely, but always possible) and all situations being safe, and about our cognitions being "wrong."

This can often play out in subtle ways, such as by providing reassurance during interoceptive exposure that the symptoms are "perfectly safe" and/or during in vivo exposure by reminding the patient that there is nothing dangerous about the situation. While often well intended, these tendencies toward providing certainty may limit the full potential of the exposure and implicitly lead the patient to think that the best way to manage their anxiety/panic is to make things more certain – as opposed to building a tolerance for uncertainty. Thus, to overcome this obstacle, the therapist should be very careful and deliberate about how they phrase their comments ("you're doing a great job in tolerating your symptoms" versus "just hang in there, you're going to be just fine, the symptoms are perfectly safe") and answer questions from the patient ("it seems like you want me to reassure you that nothing bad will happen if we enter into a crowded subway train today – can you see how this need for certainty is connected to your anxiety, and maintains it over time?").

4.6.6 Problems in the Patient–Therapist Working Alliance

A common misconception about CBT is that it is all about techniques and skills and does not pay attention to the patient–therapist working alliance. While CBT does emphasize the learning of new skills and techniques, it certainly also emphasizes building a strong working alliance with the patient that rests on being warm, nonjudgmental and respectful, empathic, genuine, flexible, and making sure that the goals and plan for reaching them are clear and collaborative. In fact, given that CBT asks patients to be willing to: (a) share and then examine their inner most troubling thoughts, and (b) face their most feared triggers, developing and then utilizing a strong working alliance is a crucial preliminary step to set up the cognitive and behavioral interventions for success.

Establishing a positive therapeutic alliance is a critical part of CBT

While in CBT, as opposed to some of the other psychotherapies, the working alliance is seen more as "necessary, but not sufficient," and numerous studies have found that the alliance correlates positively with therapeutic change across a variety of treatment modalities and clinical issues (Castonguay et al., 2006). Thus, if there are problems in the working alliance (e.g., comfort, trust, understanding, agreement on goals and plans), the treatment outcome may be compromised. To overcome this obstacle, the therapist should strive to establish, monitor, and maintain a positive bond and a strong level of collaboration with their patients and, in those instances where the working alliance quality is challenged, should be prepared to address such relationship problems, as well as to modify their approach to be responsive to their patients' needs (Castonguay et al., 2006).

4.6.7 Cognitive Therapy Techniques and Somatic Skills That Become Safety Behaviors

Another obstacle occurs when patients try to convert the cognitive interventions designed to aid them in questioning the accuracy of their beliefs into self-reassuring statements that typically revolve around creating certainty that they will be safe and that their sensations (or the situations that trigger them) are not dangerous. For example, some patients might "misuse" the psychoeducational material presented to them at the start of treatment as "proof" that there is nothing wrong with them and that nothing bad can happen. Other patients might ritualistically repeat the "rational responses" derived from formal cognitive restructuring exercises in their mind (or out loud) to distract themselves and/or reassure themselves when anxious. Finally, other patients may even carry an old "coping card" with them, that a well-intending therapist from the past had helped them to create, "just in case" they need it to keep them safe.

For similar reasons, somatic skills training (e.g., diaphragmatic breathing and progressive muscle relaxation) have been increasingly dropped from CBT protocols for panic disorder. One way to overcome these obstacles is to

Diaphragmatic breathing and progressive muscle relaxation are rarely used by contemporary therapists treating panic disorder

focus more on interoceptive and in vivo exposure and observing outcomes, and less on formal cognitive restructuring – especially before or during exposures. In addition, when doing cognitive interventions, the therapist can place the emphasis on expectancy violations and new learning that was created through the behavioral interventions. Finally, the therapist can deliberately refrain from giving the patient any certainties about their safety (after providing a rationale for doing so) and encourage the patient to embrace uncertainty, in order to build a tolerance for it, rather than avoid it, by spending the rest of their life trying to create certainty.

4.6.8 Unbearable Anxiety Levels During Exposure

On some occasions, a patient will report that they are extremely anxious (or experiencing a panic attack) during either an interoceptive or an in vivo exposure exercise, state that it is unbearable, and ask to end the exercise. To overcome this obstacle, the therapist can: (a) set up each exposure with a review of the rationale and normalization of the variability of anxiety, (b) noting any predictions about what the patient may fear will occur if faced with unbearable anxiety, (c) pause the exposure and encourage the patient to observe their anxious thoughts and sensations without trying to escape from them, or (d) end the exercise in the interest of maintaining the alliance, but then examine together the cognitions the patient had in the moment. If choosing option (d), the therapist should then try to reinitiate exposure as soon as possible, ideally by repeating the same exercise or, if necessary to reengage the patient, choosing to modify the last task to make it slightly less difficult.

4.6.9 Absence of Anxiety During Exposure

On rare occasions, a patient will report that they are experiencing little or no anxiety during an interoceptive or in vivo exposure exercise. If this occurs, it could mean that: (a) the patient feels reassured by your presence, (b) the patient is employing (or has employed in advance) subtle safety behaviors, (c) in the case of interoceptive exposure that the intensity of the exercise was not high enough and/or that they do not see the sensations as similar to their panic sensations, (d) that they are getting better and the trigger no longer makes them anxious, or (e) there are elements of the exercise that are preventing the most feared aspects of the trigger to be generated. Depending on the suspected cause, the therapist can then overcome the obstacle by: (a) altering the way the exposure exercise is performed (e.g., with the therapist not visible to the patient), (b) assessing for cognitive and behavioral safety behavior use and encouraging its removal, (c) increasing the intensity of the interoceptive exposure and/or altering it to make the symptoms more similar to the patient's naturally occurring sensations, (d) move up the hierarchy, or (e) collaborate with the patient to modify the exercise to maximize its potency to create fear.

4.7 Diversity Issues

In its most recent release of race–ethnic population estimates, the US Census Bureau estimated that nearly 4 out of 10 Americans identified with a race or ethnic group other than White and suggested that the 2010–2020 decade would be the first in the nation's history in which the White population declined in numbers (US Census Bureau, 2020). Despite the fact that: (a) minorities represent the fastest growing segment of the US population, (b) anxiety disorders appear to occur at roughly similar prevalence rates in other countries (Rego, 2009), and (c) strong evidence suggests that behavioral and cognitive behavioral approaches are particularly effective in the treatment of anxiety, there is a paucity of treatment outcome studies with all of these populations (Carter et al., 2012).

For example, in the African American population, there is evidence that exposure and CBT are effective treatment approaches, but this comes from a total of four studies. It should also be noted that each of these studies altered the treatment in some way to make it more culturally appropriate, so, to date, there have been no investigations that have relied entirely on a standard CBT treatment protocol.

Like the African American population, there has been a dearth of studies examining treatment outcomes in Asian Americans with anxiety disorders, with the few that have been done showing that Asian Americans respond to standard treatment protocols (Carter et al., 2012), but receive increased benefit and reduction in symptom severity from culturally adaptive ones (Hinton & Patel, 2017). In addition, future research will need to distinguish between different ethnic groups within the Asian American population, each with their own needs and cultural adaptations, rather than developing umbrella culturally adaptive treatments in order to try to serve them as a monolithic group with one ethnic background (Carter et al., 2012). Finally, there are at least some data suggesting that when matched with therapists of the same ethnic background, Asian Americans (as compared to European Americans, African Americans, and Mexican Americans) have a significant decrease in therapy dropout rates and number of sessions (Geiger, 1994).

Despite the exponential growth of the Latinx American population, with respect to anxiety disorders, the treatment outcome literature is sorely lacking, and very few of those have examined ethnic differences with this population (Carter et al., 2012). And the picture is even worse with respect to panic disorder: to date, there have only been two studies published examining the treatment efficacy of CBT for panic in Latinx populations. The first was an uncontrolled, single-case study published examining the treatment efficacy of a self-directed version CBT for panic disorder administered in combination with attendance in a support group for panic patients held at a local hospital (Alfonso & Dziegielewski, 2001). While the authors reported that the patient experienced a significant reduction in anxiety over the treatment phase that was maintained over a very brief (1 week) follow-up period, little can be generalized about the efficacy of CBT for panic disorder in this population from a single case study.

There has been relatively little research examining the applicability of CBT to different racial or ethnic groups

In 2016, Feldman and colleagues conducted a randomized controlled trial comparing a culturally adapted cognitive behavior psychophysiological therapy intervention to music and relaxation in 53 Latinx (primarily Puerto Rican) adults with asthma and panic disorder and found that both groups showed improvements in panic disorder severity, asthma control, and several other anxiety and asthma outcome measures from baseline to post-treatment and at 3-month follow-up. In addition, cognitive behavior psychophysiological therapy showed an advantage over music and relaxation for improvement in adherence to inhaled corticosteroids. They noted, however, that attrition was high (40%) in both groups. Finally, a substantial amount of empirical research suggests that the expression of anxiety may be different in some groups. For example, Guarnaccia et al. (2010) found that the experience of *ataque de nervios* (linked, although experientially and conceptually distinct from the experience of panic, see Cintrón et al., 2005) occurred in approximately 7–15% of the Latinx sample of the National Latino and Asian American Study.

Finally, it is worth noting that while there is at least some evidence of beneficial treatment approaches in the African American, Asian American, and Latinx American population, there is virtually no evidence (other than a very few uncontrolled trials) on the effective treatment of anxiety disorders among Native Americans (Carter et al., 2012). This is unfortunate given that some estimate that the rate of anxiety and depression is greater than 50% among Native American adults (McNeil et al., 2000).

When discussing race and ethnicity, it is important to consider related factors such as the patients' level of acculturation, socioeconomic status, access to health insurance, and other psychosocial and environmental stressors, as well as beliefs about the origin of mental illness and the meaning of their symptoms. We must also continue to evaluate: (a) the psychometric properties of all our "standard" routine outcome measures of psychopathology to ensure they are culturally adapted, (b) the influence of therapist cultural sensitivity on treatment outcome, and (c) any culturally adapted components of the standard evidence-based treatment protocols.

5

Case Vignette

Joe Smith was a 20-year-old White, heterosexual, cisgender, single male with no children, who had been employed part time while completing his second year of college. On intake, Joe reported that he experienced his first panic attack approximately 1 year prior to the time of initial assessment. He noted that he was under some stress at the time, as he was in the middle of his midterm examinations at college and had just started dating someone new. Upon further probing, he also reported that his father had died 3 months prior to his first panic attack and added that his father's death had been unexpected (the result of a sudden heart attack in an otherwise healthy man). In discussing the sudden loss of his father, Joe noted that in addition to grieving the loss, he noticed that he began to become extremely concerned about the possibility of having a heart attack himself. Although he described himself as a "somewhat anxious person" for most of his life, Joe reported that he had never experienced a panic attack before his father's death, nor had he even been particularly concerned about his health.

Joe stated that the unexpected nature of his father's death, however, produced a change in the way he thought about his own health (attentional shift) and he began to monitor himself for any possible signs of danger (i.e., an impending heart attack), as he became convinced that there "must have been some warning signals" and if he looked out closely enough, he could prevent the same thing from happening to him. Thus, from the time of his father's death to the time of his first panic attack, Joe slowly became increasingly vigilant of his own bodily sensations.

Joe recalled vividly his first panic attack, which happened "out of the blue" while he was at home, alone, on a Friday night studying for a midterm final and under some pressure to wrap up, as he had a date later that evening with a woman he had recently met. He reported suddenly feeling a sense of impending doom and noticed that his heart was racing. He got up and paced to try to "walk it off," but could not seem to relax, and thus became convinced that "this was the big one" that he had been fearing. Joe noted that he tried to "push away" the thoughts and ignore the rapidly rising sensations and feeling of anxiety, but it just seemed to get worse. Eventually, with more and more of the "classic" symptoms of a heart attack appearing (e.g., shortness of breath and dizziness) that he had frequently read about, he started to feel very ill and, fearing he would not be able to make it to the hospital, called 911. Interestingly, Joe noted that he immediately began to feel better once the emergency medical service ambulance arrived, but still agreed to go to the hospital, where he was eventually medically evaluated and cleared. It was there that he was informed he was in fine medical health, and that what he had experienced was a panic attack. He was given a benzodiazepine prescription and sent home.

Although Joe was reassured by learning he had no medical issues, he found the experience that night of the first attack so traumatic that he became convinced that he needed to "do whatever it took to never experience that feeling again." He also berated himself for waiting so long to get help that night and decided that his best bet to ward off future attacks would be to catch them as early as possible. This led Joe to become vigilant for any signs of an impending attack (e.g., chest pain, shortness of breath, nausea, sweating). From that point on, however, whenever he detected any sensations that were unusual or uncomfortable, he would interpret them to be signs of an impending attack and become very anxious. To cope, Joe would call his family and friends for support. If they were not available, Joe would then run through an "emergency coping list" he had crafted, which included trying to distract himself, pacing, taking a cold shower, and going outside for some air. If none of this seemed to help, he would go to the emergency room, "just in case." Each time he did this, however, the outcome was the same: Joe was informed that he had no medical issues and was, in fact, quite healthy. What he had experienced was a panic attack.

Over time, Joe not only became hypervigilant for signs of impending attacks but also developed high levels of anticipatory anxiety whenever he needed to enter situations in which he thought he might have a panic attack. This eventually led him to make some significant changes in his lifestyle, including ending things with the woman he had been dating and ultimately taking a leave of absence from college. In addition, Joe started to cut back on exercise and eliminated caffeine use, as he did not like the way these activities made him feel. Interestingly, while Joe also began to limit how far he would travel from home, he also did not like to be "alone with his thoughts and feelings," so he would try to distract himself while at home by doing things such as playing online video games until the emotional arousal they caused became too intense, having the television on "more watching me, than I was watching it," or napping.

By the time of his intake, Joe reported that over the year since his first attack, the frequency of panic attacks had been experiencing had been increasing from occasional to several times per week. Some of the attacks came on when expected (e.g., needing to go grocery shopping and getting "stuck" in a slow cashier lane), while others seemed to just "come on out of the blue," including when he was sleeping. He added that he felt that his life now revolved around preventing the experience of a potential panic attack, despite rationally knowing that they "likely weren't going to kill me." He added, however, that during a panic attack, the belief that he was having a heart attack seemed much more valid. To his credit, when asked, he noted that he was completely certain that most people think his beliefs were unrealistic and was very eager to consider the possibility that his beliefs may be false.

At intake, Joe met criteria for panic disorder and agoraphobia and was also subthreshold for generalized anxiety disorder. He screened negative for all other major DSM-5 disorders, including PTSD and major depressive disorder. Although he had been prescribed small quantities of a benzodiazepine after several of his emergency room visits, he noted that he had not used them, "other than once or twice to help me sleep." He was given an evidence-based pretreatment self-report assessment package focused on panic disorder and agoraphobia (e.g., PDSS-SR, ACQ, BSQ, MI), as well as one to assess and monitor the subthreshold GAD (e.g., the Penn State Worry Questionnaire [PSWQ]).

As expected, Joe's scores on the self-report assessment measures were all at or above clinical averages on the panic measures (e.g., PDSS-SR = 16 = *markedly ill*), and elevated relative to the community but below the mean for GAD patients on the measure for GAD (e.g., PSWQ = 55). Items on the BSQ indicated that Joe's most feared bodily sensations were heart palpitations, pressure, or a heavy feeling in his chest, feeling short of breath, numbness in arms or legs, and sweating. Items on the ACQ indicated that his most common panic-related thoughts were that he will have a heart attack, he is going to have a stroke, and that he is going to pass out. In his responses on the MI, Joe indicated that if he had to face them alone, he would almost always avoid or avoid most of the time the majority of places or situations, but, notably, he rated his amount of avoidance as considerably less when he was with a trusted companion.

In his favor was the fact that, at intake, Joe had embraced the idea that he had panic disorder and agoraphobia and expressed a strong motivation and commitment to "get his life back" and "face his fears head on." He added that he was now ready to "do whatever it takes" to get better, and that he had "done his research" and understood that his best shot for getting his panic and anxiety back under control was through completing a course of CBT. He was not interested in taking medication. He had read a considerable amount on what CBT was, as well as the empirical support behind CBT for panic disorder and agoraphobia. He noted that he was anxious about starting treatment, because he knew CBT was going to call on him to "face his fears," and he was desperate to get back on track in life.

Joe's treatment began with psychoeducation on the nature of panic and anxiety, as well as a presentation of the general CBT model as well as the CBT models for panic disorder and agoraphobia, and the rationale for treatment. Joe responded very well to the corrective information offer via psychoeducation; after having his symptoms explained by the CBT model, he began to understand how his beliefs about his symptoms, as well as the steps he had taken to keep himself safe, were now working against him. He was assigned self-monitoring and bibliotherapy for homework.

Cognitive restructuring was then introduced, in part because Joe expressed a genuine curiosity to learn more about how his thoughts were driving his emotions, and in part to maximize new learning while targeting Joe's physiological sensations and avoided situations via interoceptive and in vivo exposure exercises. Joe liked the cognitive restructuring techniques of decatastrophizing and probability overestimating and had never really considered his ability to cope during a panic attack. Through Socratic questioning and examining the evidence from previous panic attacks, he began to see how his fear of situations and sensations were driving him to avoid life's normal activity and how, when he ultimately had to enter his feared situations, his anticipatory anxiety generated the very bodily sensations that he had developed a hypervigilance for detecting, which, when coupled with the belief that he could not cope with it, generated the very attacks he had feared he would experience.

Joe noted, however, that while this made sense rationally, he was still afraid of experiencing the sensations and entering his feared situations. These beliefs provided an excellent rationale to transition to the interoceptive and in vivo exposure phase of treatment. In addition, to create a bridge from the cognitive restructuring to the exposure phase of treatment, Joe was asked to pay attention to the predictions he would make before each exercise, so they could be examined afterwards to facilitate new learning.

Once the interoceptive exposure phase of treatment was initiated, Joe noticed that while his sensitivity to – and concerns about – his physical sensations initially were higher, they rapidly started to diminish, both within each session and between sessions. As Joe became more comfortable with each exercise, he was instructed to challenge himself, by: (a) doing them for increasingly longer periods of time, (b) combining two of more of the exercises together (e.g., deliberate hyperventilation followed by straw breathing), (c) doing them more on his own, and (d) doing them "naturalistically." He was also asked to start drinking coffee again (which he had previously enjoyed) and return to his full exercise routine.

As Joe became more comfortable with the interoceptive exposure exercises, an interesting thing happened: He noticed that he was becoming more willing to enter situations that he had been avoiding – and had, in fact, begun to do so. He still reported high anticipatory anxiety and urges to utilize safety behaviors, however, including trying to go out at quieter times (e.g., evenings and weekends), verifying that his cell service was working and strong, and calling people to see if they wanted to accompany him (which was already an improvement over pressuring them to do so) and/or to let them know where he was going ("just in case"). Thus, an in vivo exposure hierarchy was collaboratively generated, starting with a mix of low and moderate anxiety-generating items (which allowed for accompaniment and/or initial use of safety behaviors), up to high anxiety items that required Joe to perform them on his own, without any safety behavior use. Again, an interesting thing happened: Joe quickly learned that he did not need someone to accompany him, and he began to eliminate safety behaviors on his own.

While Joe did continue to experience panic attacks during the first few weeks of treatment, which temporarily worsened when initiating interoceptive and in vivo exposure, in general the slope showed a steady decline and, by the end of treatment, he had been panic free for several weeks (despite one of his last homework assignments being to give himself a panic attack). In addition, many of Joe's negative predictions began to dissipate and, in fact, he began to express a new confidence in his ability to utilize the skills he learned in treatment when he needed them. As a result, his beliefs about the nature of anxiety and panic had shifted and he no longer saw either as threats. This new way of thinking allowed him to regain several other important aspects of his life, including a return to college and the dating scene, as well an "inner peace," whether it be when he is alone at home or out in public.

At termination, Joe was given some relapse prevention strategies and tips for managing anxiety and panic in the road ahead. He also completed the self-report assessment package that he had completed at pretreatment and, as expected, Joe's scores on all the self-report measures had decreased significantly – although were not at zero (e.g., PDSS-SR = 6 = *borderline ill* and PSWQ = 40). While he initially expressed interest in a booster session in 6 months "just in case," he identified this as a potential safety behavior and stated that he would reach out if he wanted a refresher session in the future.

6

Further Reading

Books

Abramowitz, J. S., & Blakey, S. M. (2020). *Clinical handbook of fear and anxiety: Maintenance processes and treatment mechanisms.* American Psychological Association. https://doi.org/10.1037/0000150-000
This volume highlights the key psychological processes that maintain anxiety and then describes the empirically supported mechanisms of change that are found in a variety of effective treatments and have empirical support for their effectiveness across a range of anxiety presentations.

Abramowitz, J. S., Deacon, B. J., & Whiteside, S. P. (2019). *Exposure therapy for anxiety: Principles and practice* (2nd ed.). Guilford Press.
This volume offers a detailed guide to conducting exposure therapy for anxiety, including a review of the theoretical and empirical bases and descriptions of specialized assessment and treatment planning techniques.

Clark, D. A., & Beck, A. T. (2011). *Cognitive therapy of anxiety disorders: Science and practice.* Guilford Press.
This volume synthesized the latest thinking and empirical data on anxiety treatment and offers step-by-step instructions in cognitive assessment, case formulation, cognitive restructuring, and behavioral interventions.

Barlow, D. H. & Craske, M. G. (2022). *Mastery of your anxiety and panic: Workbook* (5th ed.). Oxford University Press.
This volume has been fully revised and updated to offer patients the latest evidence-based strategies and techniques for dealing with both panic disorder and agoraphobia.

DVD/Streaming

Clark, D. M. (2007). *Cognitive therapy for panic disorder* [DVD]. APA Videos.
This video features anxiety disorder expert Dr. David Clark using several cognitive therapy techniques with a 38-year-old man with panic disorder portrayed by an actor but based on actual case material.

Wilson, R. (2012). *Cognitive therapy for panic disorder* [DVD]. Psychotherapy.net.
This video features anxiety disorder expert Dr. Reid Wilson applying a cognitive behavioral approach to panic disorder in a live session recorded with a real patient.

7

References

Addis, M. E., & Carpenter, K. M. (2000). The treatment rationale in cognitive behavioral therapy: Psychological mechanisms and clinical guidelines. *Cognitive and Behavioral Practice, 7*(2), 147–156. https://doi.org/10.1016/S1077-7229(00)80025-5

Alfonso, S., & Dziegielewski, S. F. (2001). Self-directed treatment for panic disorder: A holistic approach. *Journal of Research and Social Work Evaluation: An International Publication, 2*(1), 5–18.

Alvarez, E., Puliafico, A., Leonte, K., & Albano, A. (2021). Psychotherapy for anxiety disorders in children and adolescents. *UpToDate*. Retrieved July 4, 2021 from https://www.uptodate.com/contents/psychotherapy-for-anxiety-disorders-in-children-and-adolescents

American Psychiatric Association. (1968). *Diagnostic and statistical manual of mental disorders* (2nd ed.).

American Psychiatric Association. (1980). *Diagnostic and statistical manual of mental disorders* (3rd ed.).

American Psychiatric Association. (1987). *Diagnostic and statistical manual of mental disorders* (3rd ed., rev.).

American Psychiatric Association. (1994). *Diagnostic and statistical manual of mental disorders* (4th ed.).

American Psychiatric Association. (2009). *Practice guideline for the treatment of patients with panic disorder* (2nd ed.).

American Psychiatric Association. (2013). *Diagnostic and statistical manual of mental disorders* (5th ed.).

Amering, M., & Katschnig, H. (1990). Panic attacks and panic disorder in cross-cultural perspective. *Psychiatric Annals, 20*(9), 511–516. https://doi.org/10.3928/0048-5713-19900901-07

Antony, M. M. (2001). Measures for panic disorder and agoraphobia. In M. M. Antony, S. M. Orsillo, & L. Roemer (Eds.), *Practitioner's guide to empirically based measures of anxiety* (pp. 95–125). Kluwer Academic Publishers.

Austin, D. W., & Richards, J. C. (2001). The catastrophic misinterpretation model of panic disorder. *Behaviour Research and Therapy, 39*(11), 1277–1291. https://doi.org/10.1016/S0005-7967(00)00095-4

Baker, R., Owens, M., Thomas, S., Whittlesea, A., Abbey, G., Gower, P., Tosunlar, L., Corrigan, E., & Thomas, P. W. (2012). Does CBT facilitate emotional processing? *Behavioural and Cognitive Psychotherapy, 40*(1), 19–37. https://doi.org/10.1017/S1352465810000895

Ballenger, J. C., Pecknold, J., Rickels, K., & Sellers, E. M. (1993). Medication discontinuation in panic disorder. *Journal of Clinical Psychiatry, 54*, 15–24.

Bandelow, B., Zohar, J., Hollander, E., Kasper, S., Möller, H. J., WFSBP Task Force on Treatment Guidelines for Anxiety, Obsessive-Compulsive and Post-Traumatic Stress Disorders, Zohar, J., Hollander, E., Kasper, S., Möller, H.-J., Bandelow, B., Allgulander, C., Ayuse-Gutierrez, J., Baldwin, D. S., Buenvicius, R., Cassano, G., Fineberg, N., Gabriels, L., Hindmarch, I., ... Vega, J. (2008). World Federation of Societies of Biological Psychiatry (WFSBP) guidelines for the pharmacological treatment of anxiety, obsessive-compulsive and post-traumatic stress disorders–first revision. *World Journal of Biological Psychiatry, 9*(4), 248–312.

Barlow, D. H. (2004). *Anxiety and its disorders: The nature and treatment of anxiety and panic* (2nd ed.). Guilford Press.

Barlow, D. H., Allen, L. B., & Choate, M. L. (2004). Toward a unified treatment for emotional disorders. *Behavior Therapy, 35*, 205–230. https://doi.org/10.1016/S0005-7894(04)80036-4

Barlow, D. H., & Craske, M. G. (2006). *Mastery of your anxiety and panic* (4th ed.). Oxford University Press.

Barlow, D. H., Gorman, J. M., Shear, M. K., & Woods, S. W. (2000). Cognitive-behavioral therapy, imipramine, or their combination for panic disorder: A randomized controlled trial. *JAMA, 283*(19), 2529–2536. https://doi.org/10.1001/jama.283.19.2529

Başoglu, M., Marks, I. M., Kiliç, C., Swinson, R. P., Noshirvani, H., Kuch, K., O'Sullivan, G., & Brewin, C. R. (1994). Alprazolam and exposure for panic disorder with agoraphobia. *British Journal of Psychiatry, 164*(5), 652–659. https://doi.org/10.1192/bjp.164.5.652

Batelaan, N. M., Van Balkom, A. J., & Stein, D. J. (2012). Evidence-based pharmacotherapy of panic disorder: An update. *International Journal of Neuropsychopharmacology, 15*(3), 403–415. https://doi.org/10.1017/S1461145711000800

Beck, A. T. (1976). *Cognitive therapy and the emotional disorders*. Penguin.

Beck, A. T. (1988). Cognitive approaches to panic disorder: Theory and therapy. In S. Rachman & J. D. Maser (Eds.), *Panic: Psychological perspectives* (pp. 91–109). Lawrence Erlbaum Associates.

Beesdo, K., Knappe, S., & Pine, D. S. (2009). Anxiety and anxiety disorders in children and adolescents: Developmental issues and implications for DSM-V. *Psychiatric Clinics of North America, 32*(3), 483–524. https://doi.org/10.1016/j.psc.2009.06.002

Beghi, E., Allais, G., Cortelli, P., D'Amico, D., De Simone, R., d'Onofrio, F., Genco, S., Manzoni, G. C., Moschiano, F., Tonini, M. C., Torelli, P., Quartaroli, M., Roncolato, M., Salvi, S., & Bussone, G. (2007). Headache and anxiety-depressive disorder comorbidity: The HADAS study. *Neurological Sciences, 28*(2), S217–S219.

Blakey, S. M., Abramowitz, J. S., Buchholz, J. L., Jessup, S. C., Jacoby, R. J., Reuman, L., & Pentel, K. Z. (2019). A randomized controlled trial of the judicious use of safety behaviors during exposure therapy. *Behaviour Research and Therapy, 112*, 28–35. https://doi.org/10.1016/j.brat.2018.11.010

Bögels, S. M., & Mansell, W. (2004). Attention processes in the maintenance and treatment of social phobia: Hypervigilance, avoidance and self-focused attention. *Clinical Psychology Review, 24*, 827–856. https://doi.org/10.1016/j.cpr.2004.06.005

Bouton, M. E., Mineka, S., & Barlow, D. H. (2001). A modern learning theory perspective on the etiology of panic disorder. *Psychological Review, 108*(1), 4–32. https://doi.org/10.1037/0033-295X.108.1.4

Brown, T. A., & Barlow, D. H. (2014a). *Anxiety and Related Disorders Interview Schedule for DSM-5 (ADIS-5): Adult version*. Oxford University Press.

Brown, T. A., & Barlow, D. H. (2014b). *Anxiety and Related Disorders Interview Schedule for DSM-5 (ADIS-5L): Lifetime version*. Oxford University Press.

Bruijniks, S. J. E., DeRubeis, R. J., Hollon, S. D., & Huibers, M. J. H. (2019). The potential role of learning capacity in cognitive behavior therapy for depression: A systematic review of the evidence and future directions for improving therapeutic learning. *Clinical Psychological Science, 7*(4), 668–692. https://doi.org/10.1177/2167702619830391

Buckley, P. F., Miller, B. J., Lehrer, D. S., & Castle, D. J. (2009). Psychiatric comorbidities and schizophrenia. *Schizophrenia Bulletin, 35*(2), 383–402. https://doi.org/10.1093/schbul/sbn135

Butler, A. C., Chapman, J. E., Forman, E. M., & Beck, A. T. (2006). The empirical status of cognitive-behavioral therapy: A review of meta-analyses. *Clinical Psychology Review, 26*(1), 17–31. https://doi.org/10.1016/j.cpr.2005.07.003

Bystritsky, A., Kerwin, L., Niv, N., Natoli, J. L., Abrahami, N., Klap, R., Wells, K., & Young, A. S. (2010). Clinical and subthreshold panic disorder. *Depression and Anxiety, 27*(4), 381–389. https://doi.org/10.1002/da.20622

Caldirola, D., De Donatis, D., Alciati, A., Daccò, S., & Perna, G. (2023). Pharmacological approaches to the management of panic disorder in older patients: A systematic review. *Expert Review of Neurotherapeutics*, 1-17. https://doi.org/10.1080/14737175.2023.2254938

Carleton, R. N. (2012). The intolerance of uncertainty construct in the context of anxiety disorders: Theoretical and practical perspectives. *Expert review of neurotherapeutics, 12*(8), 937-947. https://doi.org/10.1586/ern.12.82

Carleton, R. N., Mulvogue, M. K., Thibodeau, M. A., McCabe, R. E., Antony, M. M., & Asmundson, G. J. (2012). Increasingly certain about uncertainty: Intolerance of uncertainty across anxiety and depression. *Journal of anxiety disorders, 26*(3), 468-479. https://doi.org/10.1016/j.janxdis.2012.01.011

Carter, M. M., Mitchell, F. E., & Sbrocco, T. (2012). Treating ethnic minority adults with anxiety disorders: Current status and future recommendations. *Journal of Anxiety Disorders, 26*(4), 488-501. https://doi.org/10.1016/j.janxdis.2012.02.002

Castonguay, L. G., Constantino, M. J., & Holtforth, M. G. (2006). The working alliance: Where are we and where should we go? *Psychotherapy: Theory, Research, Practice, Training, 43*(3), 271-279. https://doi.org/10.1037/0033-3204.43.3.271

Chambless, D. L., Caputo, G. C., Bright, P., & Gallagher, R. (1984). Assessment of fear of fear in agoraphobics: The body sensations questionnaire and the agoraphobic cognitions questionnaire. *Journal of Consulting and Clinical Psychology, 52*(6), 1090-1097. https://doi.org/10.1037/0022-006X.52.6.1090

Chambless, D. L., Caputo, G. C., Jasin, S. E., Gracely, E. J., & Williams, C. (1985). The Mobility Inventory for Agoraphobia. *Behaviour Research and Therapy, 23*(1), 35-44. https://doi.org/10.1016/0005-7967(85)90140-8

Chawla, N., Anothaisintawee, T., Charoenrungrueangchai, K., Thaipisuttikul, P., McKay, G. J., Attia, J., & Thakkinstian, A. (2022). Drug treatment for panic disorder with or without agoraphobia: Systematic review and network meta-analysis of randomised controlled trials. *BMJ, 376*, Article e066084. https://doi.org/10.1136/bmj-2021-066084

Chen, Y. H., Hu, C. J., Lee, H. C., & Lin, H. C. (2010). An increased risk of stroke among panic disorder patients: A 3-year follow-up study. *Canadian Journal of Psychiatry, 55*(1), 43-49. https://doi.org/10.1177/070674371005500107

Cintrón, J. A., Carter, M. M., & Sbrocco, T. (2005). Ataques de nervios in relation to anxiety sensitivity among island Puerto Ricans. *Culture, Medicine and Psychiatry, 29*(4), 415-431. https://doi.org/10.1007/s11013-006-9001-7

Clark, D. M. (1986). A cognitive approach to panic. *Behaviour Research and Therapy, 24*(4), 461-470. https://doi.org/10.1016/0005-7967(86)90011-2

Clark, D. M. (1988). A cognitive model of panic attacks. In S. Rachman & J. D. Maser (Eds.), *Panic: Psychological perspectives* (pp. 71-89). Lawrence Erlbaum Associates.

Clark, D. M., & Salkovskis, P. M. (1987). *Cognitive treatment for panic attacks: Therapist's manual*. Department of Psychiatry, University of Oxford.

Clark, D. M., Salkovskis, P. M., Gelder, M. G., Koehler, C., Martin, M., Anastasiades, P., Hackmann, A., Middleton, H., & Jeavons, A. (1988). Tests of a cognitive theory of panic. In I. Hand & H.-U. Wittchen (Eds.), *Panic and phobias 2: Treatments and variables affecting course and outcome* (pp. 149-158). Springer. https://doi.org/10.1007/978-3-642-73543-1_13

Clum, G. A., & Knowles, S. L. (1991). Why do some people with panic disorders become avoidant? A review. *Clinical Psychology Review, 11*, 295-313. https://doi.org/10.1016/0272-7358(91)90105-4

Comer, J. S., Hong, N., Poznanski, B., Silva, K., & Wilson, M. (2019). Evidence base update on the treatment of early childhood anxiety and related problems. *Journal of Clinical Child and Adolescent Psychology, 48*(1), 1-15. https://doi.org/10.1080/15374416.2018.1534208

Cooper-Patrick, L., Powe, N. R., Jenckes, M. W., Gonzales, J. J., Levine, D. M., & Ford, D. E. (1997). Identification of patient attitudes and preferences regarding treatment of depression. *Journal of General Internal Medicine, 12*(7), 431-438. https://doi.org/10.1046/j.1525-1497.1997.00075.x

Cox, B. J., Fergus, K. D., & Swinson, R. P. (1994). Patient satisfaction with behavioral treatments for panic disorder with agoraphobia. *Journal of Anxiety Disorders, 8*(3), 193-206. https://doi.org/10.1016/0887-6185(94)90001-9

Cox, B. J., Norton, G. R., Swinson, R. P., & Endler, N. S. (1990). Substance abuse and panic-related anxiety: A critical review. *Behaviour Research and Therapy, 28*(5), 385-393. https://doi.org/10.1016/0005-7967(90)90157-E

Craske, M. G., & Rowe, M. K. (1997). Nocturnal panic. *Clinical Psychology: Science and Practice, 4*(2), 153-174. https://doi.org/10.1111/j.1468-2850.1997.tb00107.x

Craske, M. G., Kircanski, K., Zelikowsky, M., Mystkowski, J., Chowdhury, N., & Baker, A. (2008). Optimizing inhibitory learning during exposure therapy. *Behaviour Research and Therapy, 46*(1), 5-27. https://doi.org/10.1016/j.brat.2007.10.003

Craske, M. G., Liao, B., Brown, L., & Vervliet, B. (2012). Role of inhibition in exposure therapy. *Journal of Experimental Psychopathology, 3*(3), 322-345. https://doi.org/10.5127/jep.026511

Craske, M. G., Treanor, M., Conway, C. C., Zbozinek, T., & Vervliet, B. (2014). Maximizing exposure therapy: An inhibitory learning approach. *Behaviour Research and Therapy, 58*, 10-23. https://doi.org/10.1016/j.brat.2014.04.006

Doyle, A., & Pollack, M. H. (2004). Long-term management of panic disorder. *Journal of Clinical Psychiatry, 65*(Suppl. 5), 24-28.

Fava, G. A., Zielezny, M., Savron, G., & Grandi, S. (1995). Long-term effects of behavioural treatment for panic disorder with agoraphobia. *British Journal of Psychiatry, 166*(1), 87-92. https://doi.org/10.1192/bjp.166.1.87

Feldman, J. M., Matte, L., Interian, A., Lehrer, P. M., Lu, S.-E., Scheckner, B., Steinbert, D. M., Oken, T., Kotay, A., Sinha, S., & Shim, C. (2016). Psychological treatment of comorbid asthma and panic disorder in Latino adults: Results from a randomized controlled trial. *Behaviour Research and Therapy, 87*, 142-154. https://doi.org/10.1016/j.brat.2016.09.007

Fenn, K., & Byrne, M. (2013). The key principles of cognitive behavioural therapy. *InnovAiT, 6*(9), 579-585. https://doi.org/10.1177/1755738012471029

First, M. B., Williams, J. B. W., Karg, R. S., & Spitzer, R. L. (2015). *Structured Clinical Interview for DSM-5: Research version (SCID-5 for DSM-5, research version; SCID-5-RV)*. American Psychiatric Association.

First, M. B., Williams, J. B. W., Karg, R. S., & Spitzer, R. L. (2016). *Structured Clinical Interview for DSM-5 Disorders: Clinician version (SCID-5-CV)*. American Psychiatric Association.

Fleet, R., Lespérance, F., Arsenault, A., Grégoire, J., Lavoie, K., Laurin, C., Harel, F., Burelle, D., Lambert, J., Beitman, B., & Frasure-Smith, N. (2005). Myocardial perfusion study of panic attacks in patients with coronary artery disease. *American Journal of Cardiology, 96*(8), 1064-1068. https://doi.org/10.1016/j.amjcard.2005.06.035

Foa, E. B., & Kozak, M. J. (1986). Emotional processing of fear: Exposure to corrective information. *Psychological Bulletin, 99*(1), 20-35. https://doi.org/10.1037/0033-2909.99.1.20

Foa, E. B., Franklin, M. E., & Moser, J. (2002). Context in the clinic: How well do cognitive-behavioral therapies and medications work in combination? *Biological Psychiatry, 52*(10), 987-997. https://doi.org/10.1016/S0006-3223(02)01552-4

Foa, E. B., & McNally, R. J. (1996). Mechanisms of change in exposure therapy. In R. M. Rapee (Ed.), *Current controversies in the anxiety disorders* (pp. 329-343). Guilford Press.

Funayama, T., Furukawa, T. A., Nakano, Y., Noda, Y., Ogawa, S., Watanabe, N., Chen, J., & Noguchi, Y. (2013). In-situation safety behaviors among patients with panic disorder: Descriptive and correlational study. *Psychiatry and Clinical Neurosciences, 67*(5), 332-339. https://doi.org/10.1111/pcn.12061

Furukawa, T. A., Watanabe, N., & Churchill, R. (2007). Combined psychotherapy plus antidepressants for panic disorder with or without agoraphobia. *Cochrane Database of Systematic Reviews*. https://doi.org/10.1002/14651858.CD004364.pub2

Gearing, R. E., Schwalbe, C. S., Lee, R., & Hoagwood, K. E. (2013). The effectiveness of booster sessions in CBT treatment for child and adolescent mood and anxiety disorders. *Depression and anxiety, 30*(9), 800-808. https://doi.org/10.1002/da.22118

Geiger, L. A. (1994). *Ethnic match and client characteristics as predictors of treatment outcome for anxiety disorders* [Unpublished doctoral dissertation]. Fuller Theological Seminary.

Gelkopf, M., & Kreitler, S. (1996). Is humor only fun, an alternative cure or magic? The cognitive therapeutic potential of humor. *Journal of Cognitive Psychotherapy, 10*(4), 235-254. https://doi.org/10.1891/0889-8391.10.4.235

Gomez-Caminero, A., Blumentals, W. A., Russo, L. J., Brown, R. R., & Castilla-Puentes, R. (2005). Does panic disorder increase the risk of coronary heart disease? A cohort study of a national managed care database. *Psychosomatic Medicine, 67*(5), 688-691. https://doi.org/10.1097/01.psy.0000174169.14227.1f

Goodwin, R. D. (2003). The prevalence of panic attacks in the United States: 1980 to 1995. *Journal of Clinical Epidemiology, 56*(9), 914-916. https://doi.org/10.1016/S0895-4356(03)00126-4

Goodwin, R. D., Weinberger, A. H., Kim, J. H., Wu, M., & Galea, S. (2020). Trends in anxiety among adults in the United States, 2008-2018: Rapid increases among young adults. *Journal of Psychiatric Research, 130*, 441-446. https://doi.org/10.1016/j.jpsychires.2020.08.014

Gould, R. A., Otto, M. W., & Pollack, M. H. (1995). A meta-analysis of treatment outcome for panic disorder. *Clinical Psychology Review, 15*(8), 819-844. https://doi.org/10.1016/0272-7358(95)00048-8

Guarnaccia, P. J., Lewis-Fernandez, R., Martinez Pincay, I., Shrout, P., Guo, J., Torres, M., Canino, G., & Alegria, M. (2010). Ataque de nervios as a marker of social and psychiatric vulnerability: Results from the NLAAS. *International Journal of Social Psychiatry, 56*(3), 298-309. https://doi.org/10.1177/0020764008101636

Hall, C. L., Moldavsky, M., Baldwin, L., Marriott, M., Newell, K., Taylor, J., Sayal, K., & Hollis, C. (2013). The use of routine outcome measures in two child and adolescent mental health services: A completed audit cycle. *BMC Psychiatry, 13*, 270. https://doi.org/10.1186/1471-244X-13-270

Ham, P., Waters, D. B., & Oliver, M. N. (2005). Treatment of panic disorder. *American Family Physician, 71*(4), 733-739.

Hasler, G., Gergen, P. J., Kleinbaum, D. G., Ajdacic, V., Gamma, A., Eich, D., Rössler, W., & Angst, J. (2005). Asthma and panic in young adults: A 20-year prospective community study. *American Journal of Respiratory and Critical Care Medicine, 171*(11), 1224-1230. https://doi.org/10.1164/rccm.200412-1669OC

Hazlett-Stevens, H., Craske, M. G., Roy-Byrne, P. P., Sherbourne, C. D., Stein, M. B., & Bystritsky, A. (2002). Predictors of willingness to consider medication and psychosocial treatment for panic disorder in primary care patients. *General Hospital Psychiatry, 24*(5), 316-321. https://doi.org/10.1016/S0163-8343(02)00204-9

Heuer, L. E., Mathew, S. J., & Charney, D. S. (2009). Panic disorder. In L. R. Squire (Ed.), *Encyclopedia of Neuroscience* (pp. 421-425). Elsevier. https://doi.org/10.1016/B978-008045046-9.00392-2

Hibbert, G. A. (1984). Ideational components of anxiety: Their origin and content. *British Journal of Psychiatry, 144*(6), 618-624. https://doi.org/10.1192/bjp.144.6.618

Higa-McMillan, C. K., Francis, S. E., Rith-Najarian, L., & Chorpita, B. F. (2016). Evidence base update: 50 Years of research on treatment for child and adolescent anxiety. *Journal of Clinical Child and Adolescent Psychology, 45*(2), 91-113. https://doi.org/10.1080/15374416.2015.1046177

Hinton, D. E., & Patel, A. (2017). Cultural adaptations of cognitive behavioral therapy. *Psychiatric Clinics, 40*(4), 701-714. https://doi.org/10.1016/j.psc.2017.08.006

Hofmann, S. G., & Hinton, D. E. (2014). Cross-cultural aspects of anxiety disorders. *Current Psychiatry Reports, 16*(6), 450. https://doi.org/10.1007/s11920-014-0450-3

Holt, R. L., & Lydiard, R. B. (2007). Management of treatment-resistant panic disorder. *Psychiatry (Edgmont), 4*(10), 48.

Jakubovski, E., & Bloch, M. H. (2016). Anxiety disorder-specific predictors of treatment outcome in the coordinated anxiety learning and management (CALM) trial. *Psychiatric Quarterly, 87*(3), 445–464. https://doi.org/10.1007/s11126-015-9399-6

Kaiya, H., Sugaya, N., Iwasa, R., & Tochigi, M. (2008). Characteristics of fatigue in panic disorder patients. *Psychiatry and Clinical Neurosciences, 62*(2), 234–237. https://doi.org/10.1111/j.1440-1819.2008.01760.x

Katzman, M. A., Bleau, P., Blier, P., Chokka, P., Kjernisted, K., & Van Ameringen, M. (2014). Canadian clinical practice guidelines for the management of anxiety, posttraumatic stress and obsessive-compulsive disorders. *BMC Psychiatry, 14*(1), 1–83. https://doi.org/10.1186/1471-244X-14-S1-S1

Keijsers, G. P., Kampman, M., & Hoogduin, C. A. (2001). Dropout prediction in cognitive behavior therapy for panic disorder. *Behavior Therapy, 32*(4), 739–749. https://doi.org/10.1016/S0005-7894(01)80018-6

Kendall, P. C., Gosch, E., Furr, J. M., & Sood, E. (2008). Flexibility within fidelity. *Journal of the American Academy of Child & Adolescent Psychiatry, 47*(9), 987–993. https://doi.org/10.1097/CHI.0b013e31817eed2f

Kessler, R. C., Berglund, P., Demler, O., Jin, R., Merikangas, K. R., & Walters, E. E. (2005). Lifetime prevalence and age-of-onset distributions of DSM-IV disorders in the National Comorbidity Survey Replication. *Archives of General Psychiatry, 62*(6), 593–602. https://doi.org/10.1001/archpsyc.62.6.593

Kessler, R. C., Chiu, W. T., Demler, O., & Walters, E. E. (2005). Prevalence, severity, and comorbidity of 12-month DSM-IV disorders in the National Comorbidity Survey Replication. *Archives of General Psychiatry, 62*(6), 617–627. https://doi.org/10.1001/archpsyc.62.6.617

Kessler, R. C., Chiu, W. T., Jin, R., Ruscio, A. M., Shear, K., & Walters, E. E. (2006). The epidemiology of panic attacks, panic disorder, and agoraphobia in the National Comorbidity Survey Replication. *Archives of General Psychiatry, 63*(4), 415–424. https://doi.org/10.1001/archpsyc.63.4.415

King, B. R., & Boswell, J. F. (2019). Therapeutic strategies and techniques in early cognitive-behavioral therapy. *Psychotherapy, 56*(1), 35. https://doi.org/10.1037/pst0000202

Keogh, E., & Asmundson, G. J. (2004). Negative affectivity, catastrophizing, and anxiety sensitivity. *Understanding and treating fear of pain, 91*, 115. https://doi.org/10.1093/oso/9780198525141.003.0005

Leahy, R. L. (2001). *Overcoming resistance in cognitive therapy*. Guilford Press.

LeBeau, R. T., Davies, C. D., Culver, N. C., & Craske, M. G. (2013). Homework compliance counts in cognitive-behavioral therapy. *Cognitive Behaviour Therapy, 42*(3), 171–179. https://doi.org/10.1080/16506073.2013.763286

Lee, H. B., Hening, W. A., Allen, R. P., Kalaydjian, A. E., Earley, C. J., Eaton, W. W., & Lyketsos, C. G. (2008). Restless legs syndrome is associated with DSM-IV major depressive disorder and panic disorder in the community. *Journal of Neuropsychiatry and Clinical Neurosciences, 20*(1), 101–105. https://doi.org/10.1176/jnp.2008.20.1.101

Lee, M., Lu, W., Mann-Barnes, T., Nam, J. H., Nelson, J., & Ma, G. X. (2021). Mental health screening needs and preference in treatment types and providers in African American and Asian American older adults. *Brain Sciences, 11*(5), 597–607. https://doi.org/10.3390/brainsci11050597

Levy, H. C., & Radomsky, A. S. (2014). Safety behaviour enhances the acceptability of exposure. *Cognitive Behaviour Therapy, 43*(1), 83–92. https://doi.org/10.1080/16506073.2013.819376

Lochner, C., Mogotsi, M., du Toit, P. L., Kaminer, D., Niehaus, D. J., & Stein, D. J. (2003). Quality of life in anxiety disorders: A comparison of obsessive-compulsive disorder, social anxiety disorder, and panic disorder. *Psychopathology, 36*(5), 255–262. https://doi.org/10.1159/000073451

Marchesi, C. (2008). Pharmacological management of panic disorder. *Neuropsychiatric Disease and Treatment, 4*(1), 93-106. https://doi.org/10.2147/NDT.S1557

Margraf, J., Barlow, D. H., Clark, D. M., & Telch, M. J. (1993). Psychological treatment of panic: Work in progress on outcome, active ingredients, and follow-up. *Behaviour Research and Therapy, 31*(1), 1-8. https://doi.org/10.1016/0005-7967(93)90036-T

Marks, I. M., Swinson, R. P., Başoğlu, M., Kuch, K., Noshirvani, H., O'Sullivan, G., Lelliot, P. T., Kirby, M., McNamee, G., Sengun, S., & Wickwire, K. (1993). Alprazolam and exposure alone and combined in panic disorder with agoraphobia: A controlled study in London and Toronto. *British Journal of Psychiatry, 162*(6), 776-787. https://doi.org/10.1192/bjp.162.6.776

Maron, E., & Shlik, J. (2006). Serotonin function in panic disorder: Important, but why? *Neuropsychopharmacology, 31*(1), 1-11. https://doi.org/10.1038/sj.npp.1300880

McCabe, R. E. (2015). Subjective units of distress scale. *Phobias: The Psychology of Irrational Fear, 18*, 361.

McEvoy, P. M., & Erceg-Hurn, D. M. (2016). The search for universal transdiagnostic and trans-therapy change processes: Evidence for intolerance of uncertainty. *Journal of anxiety disorders, 41*, 96-107. https://doi.org/10.1016/j.janxdis.2016.02.002

McHugh, R. K., Whitton, S. W., Peckham, A. D., Welge, J. A., & Otto, M. W. (2013). Patient preference for psychological vs pharmacologic treatment of psychiatric disorders: A meta-analytic review. *Journal of Clinical Psychiatry, 74*(6), 595-602. https://doi.org/10.4088/JCP.12r07757

McNeil, D. W., Porter, C. A., Zvolensky, M. J., Chaney, J. M., & Kee, M. (2000). Assessment of culturally related anxiety in American Indians and Alaska Natives. *Behavior Therapy, 31*(2), 301-325. https://doi.org/10.1016/S0005-7894(00)80017-9

Mersch, P. P. A., Emmelkamp, P. M., & Lips, C. (1991). Social phobia: Individual response patterns and the long-term effects of behavioral and cognitive interventions. A follow-up study. *Behaviour Research and Therapy, 29*(4), 357-362. https://doi.org/10.1016/0005-7967(91)90072-B

Meuret, A. E., Kroll, J., & Ritz, T. (2017). Panic disorder comorbidity with medical conditions and treatment implications. *Annual Review of Clinical Psychology, 13*, 209-240. https://doi.org/10.1146/annurev-clinpsy-021815-093044

Micco, J. A., Choate-Summers, M. L., Ehrenreich, J. T., Pincus, D. B., & Mattis, S. G. (2007). Identifying efficacious treatment components of panic control treatment for adolescents: A preliminary examination. *Child & Family Behavior Therapy, 29*(4), 1-23. https://doi.org/10.1300/J019v29n04_01

Miller, W. R., & Rose, G. S. (2015). Motivational interviewing and decisional balance: Contrasting responses to client ambivalence. *Behavioural and Cognitive Psychotherapy, 43*(2), 129-141. https://doi.org/10.1017/S1352465813000878

Mitte, K. (2005). A meta-analysis of the efficacy of psycho- and pharmacotherapy in panic disorder with and without agoraphobia. *Journal of Affective Disorders, 88*(1), 27-45. https://doi.org/10.1016/j.jad.2005.05.003

Montejo-Gonzalez, A. L., Llorca, G., Izquierdo, J. A., Ledesma, A., Bousoño, M., Calcedo, A., Caarrasco, J. L., Ciudad, J., Daniel, E., De la Gandara, J., Derecho, J., Franco, M., Gomez, M. J., Macias, J. A., Martin, T., Perez, V., Sanchez, J. M., Sanchez, S., & Vicens, E. (1997). SSRI-induced sexual dysfunction: Fluoxetine, paroxetine, sertraline, and fluvoxamine in a prospective, multicenter, and descriptive clinical study of 344 patients. *Journal of Sex and Marital Therapy, 23*, 176-194.

Neumeister, A., Daher, R. J., & Charney, D. S. (2005). Anxiety disorders: Noradrenergic neurotransmission. *Anxiety and Anxiolytic Drugs*, 205-223. https://doi.org/10.1007/3-540-28082-0_8

National Institute for Mental Health. (2022). *Panic disorder: When fear overwhelms.* https://www.nimh.nih.gov/health/publications/panic-disorder-when-fear-overwhelms

Newman, M. G. (2000). Generalized anxiety disorder. In M. Hersen & M. Biaggio (Eds.), *Effective brief therapies: A clinician's guide* (pp. 157-178). Academic Press.

Newman, M. G., & Llera, S. J. (2011). A novel theory of experiential avoidance in generalized anxiety disorder: A review and synthesis of research supporting a contrast avoidance model of worry. *Clinical Psychology Review, 31*, 371-382. https://doi.org/10.1016/j.cpr.2011.01.008

Ninan, P. T., & Dunlop, B. W. (2005). Neurobiology and etiology of panic disorder. *Journal of Clinical Psychiatry, 66*(Suppl. 4), 3-7.

Oei, T. P., Llamas, M., & Devilly, G. J. (1999). The efficacy and cognitive processes of cognitive behaviour therapy in the treatment of panic disorder with agoraphobia. *Behavioural and Cognitive Psychotherapy, 27*(1), 63-88. https://doi.org/10.1017/S1352465899271081

Otto, M. W., Pollack, M. H., & Maki, K. M. (2000). Empirically supported treatments for panic disorder: Costs, benefits, and stepped care. *Journal of Consulting and Clinical Psychology, 68*(4), 556. https://doi.org/10.1037/0022-006X.68.4.556

Otto, M. W., Pollack, M. H., Sachs, G. S., Reiter, S. R., Meltzer-Brody, S., & Rosenbaum, J. F. (1993). Discontinuation of benzodiazepine treatment: Efficacy of cognitive-behavioral therapy. *American Journal of Psychiatry, 150*(10), 1485-1490. https://doi.org/10.1176/ajp.150.10.1485

Papola, D., Ostuzzi, G., Gastaldon, C., Purgato, M., Del Giovane, C., Pompoli, A., Karyotaki, E., Sijbrandij, M., Furukawa, T. A., Cuijpers, P., & Barbui, C. (2020). Which psychotherapy is effective in panic disorder? And which delivery formats are supported by the evidence? Study protocol for two systematic reviews and network meta-analyses. *BMJ Open, 10*(12), e038909.

Papola, D., Ostuzzi, G., Tedeschi, F., Gastaldon, C., Purgato, M., Del Giovane, C., Pompoli, A., Pauley, D., Karyotaki, E., Sijbrandij, M., Furukawa, T. A., Cuijpers, P., & Barbui, C. (2022). Comparative efficacy and acceptability of psychotherapies for panic disorder with or without agoraphobia: Systematic review and network meta-analysis of randomised controlled trials. *British Journal of Psychiatry, 221*(3), 507-519.

Penava, S. J., Otto, M. W., Maki, K. M., & Pollack, M. H. (1998). Rate of improvement during cognitive-behavioral group treatment for panic disorder. *Behaviour Research and Therapy, 36*(7-8), 665-673. https://doi.org/10.1016/S0005-7967(98)00035-7

Pilowsky, D. J., Olfson, M., Gameroff, M. J., Wickramaratne, P., Blanco, C., Feder, A., Gross, R., Neria, Y., & Weissman, M. M. (2006). Panic disorder and suicidal ideation in primary care. *Depression and Anxiety, 23*(1), 11-16. https://doi.org/10.1002/da.20092

Pincus, D. B., May, J. E., Whitton, S. W., Mattis, S. G., & Barlow, D. H. (2010). Cognitive-behavioral treatment of panic disorder in adolescence. *Journal of Clinical Child & Adolescent Psychology, 39*(5), 638-649. https://doi.org/10.1080/15374416.2010.501288

Pollack, M. H., Otto, M. W., Kaspi, S. P., Hammerness, P. G., & Rosenbaum, J. F. (1994). Cognitive behavior therapy for treatment-refractory panic disorder. *Journal of Clinical Psychiatry, 55*(5), 200-205.

Pompoli, A., Furukawa, T. A., Efthimiou, O., Imai, H., Tajika, A., & Salanti, G. (2018). Dismantling cognitive-behaviour therapy for panic disorder: a systematic review and component network meta-analysis. *Psychological medicine, 48*(12), 1945-1953. https://doi.org/10.1017/S0033291717003919

Powers, M. B., Zum Vörde Sive Vörding, M., Sanders, C., & Emmelkamp, P. (n.d.). *The nature and causes of anxiety and panic*. https://drkevinchapman.com/wp-content/uploads/2016/12/Powers_NatureCausesPanic.pdf

Pull, C. B., & Damsa, C. (2008). Pharmacotherapy of panic disorder. *Neuropsychiatric Disease and Treatment, 4*, 779-795. https://doi.org/10.2147/NDT.S1224

Rachman, S., Radomsky, A. S., & Shafran, R. (2008). Safety behaviour: A reconsideration. *Behaviour Research and Therapy, 46*(2), 163-173. https://doi.org/10.1016/j.brat.2007.11.008

Rego, S. A. (2009). Culture and anxiety disorders. In S. Eshun and R. Gurung (Eds.), *Culture and mental health: Sociocultural influences, theory, and practice* (pp. 197-220). Wiley-Blackwell Publishing.

Rosser, B. A. (2019). Intolerance of uncertainty as a transdiagnostic mechanism of psychological difficulties: A systematic review of evidence pertaining to causality and temporal precedence. *Cognitive therapy and research, 43*(2), 438-463. https://doi.org/10.1007/s10608-018-9964-z

Salkovskis, P. M. (1988). Phenomenology, assessment, and the cognitive model of panic. In S. Rachman & J. D. Maser (Eds.), *Panic: Psychological perspectives* (pp. 111-136). Lawrence Erlbaum Associates.

Salkovskis, P. M., & Clark, D. M. (1986). Cognitive and Physiological Processes in the Maintainance and Treatment of Panic Attacks. In *Panic and Phobias: Empirical Evidence of Theoretical Models and Longterm Effects of Behavioral Treatments* (pp. 90-103). Berlin, Heidelberg: Springer Berlin Heidelberg. https://doi.org/10.1007/978-3-642-71165-7_10

Salkovskis, P. M., & Clark, D. M. (1990). Affective responses to hyperventilation: A test of the cognitive model of panic. *Behaviour Research and Therapy, 28*(1), 51-61. https://doi.org/10.1016/0005-7967(90)90054-M

Salkovskis, P. M., Clark, D. M., & Hackmann, A. (1991). Treatment of panic attacks using cognitive therapy without exposure or breathing retraining. *Behaviour Research and Therapy, 29*(2), 161-166. https://doi.org/10.1016/0005-7967(91)90044-4

Salkovskis, P. M., Hackmann, A., Wells, A., Gelder, M. G., & Clark, D. M. (2007). Belief disconfirmation versus habituation approaches to situational exposure in panic disorder with agoraphobia: A pilot study. *Behaviour Research and Therapy, 45*(5), 877-885. https://doi.org/10.1016/j.brat.2006.02.008

Sanderson, W. C., Rapee, R. M., & Barlow, D. H. (1989). The influence of an illusion of control on panic attacks induced via inhalation of 5.5% carbon dioxide-enriched air. *Archives of General Psychiatry, 46*(2), 157-162. https://doi.org/10.1001/archpsyc.1989.01810020059010

Sanderson, W. C., & Wetzler, S. (1990). Five percent carbon dioxide challenge: Valid analogue and marker of panic disorder? *Biological Psychiatry, 27*(7), 689-701. https://doi.org/10.1016/0006-3223(90)90584-O

Saper, B. (1987). Humor in psychotherapy: Is it good or bad for the client? *Professional Psychology: Research and Practice, 18*(4), 360. https://doi.org/10.1037/0735-7028.18.4.360

Sheehan, D. V., Lecrubier, Y., Harnett-Sheehan, K., Amorim, P., Janavs, J., Weiller, E., Hergueta, T., Baker, R., & Dunbar, G. (1998). The Mini International Neuropsychiatric Interview (M.I.N.I.): The development and validation of a structured diagnostic psychiatric interview. *Journal of Clinical Psychiatry, 59*(Suppl. 20), 22-33. https://doi.org/10.1037/t18597-000

Somers, J. M., Goldner, E. M., Waraich, P., & Hsu, L. (2006). Prevalence and incidence studies of anxiety disorders: A systematic review of the literature. *Canadian Journal of Psychiatry, 51*(2), 100-113. https://doi.org/10.1177/070674370605100206

Starcevic, V., Latas, M., Kolar, D., & Berle, D. (2007). Are there gender differences in catastrophic appraisals in panic disorder with agoraphobia? *Depression and Anxiety, 24*(8), 545-552. https://doi.org/10.1002/da.20245

Sullivan, G. M., Kent, J. M., Kleber, M., Martinez, J. M., Yeragani, V. K., & Gorman, J. M. (2004). Effects of hyperventilation on heart rate and QT variability in panic disorder pre-and post-treatment. *Psychiatry Research, 125*(1), 29-39. https://doi.org/10.1016/j.psychres.2003.10.002

Swift, J. K., Callahan, J. L., Cooper, M., & Parkin, S. R. (2019). Preferences. In J. C. Norcross & B. E. Wampold (Eds.), *Psychotherapy relationships that work: Evidence-based therapist responsiveness* (pp. 157-187). Oxford University Press.

Szuhany, K. L., & Simon, N. M. (2022). Anxiety disorders: A review. *JAMA: Journal of the American Medical Association, 328*(24), 2431-2445.

Tagalidou, N., Distlberger, E., Loderer, V., & Laireiter, A. R. (2019). Efficacy and feasibility of a humor training for people suffering from depression, anxiety, and adjustment disorder: A randomized controlled trial. *BMC Psychiatry, 19*(1), 1-13. https://doi.org/10.1186/s12888-019-2075-x

Teachman, B. A., Marker, C. D., & Clerkin, E. M. (2010). Catastrophic misinterpretations as a predictor of symptom change during treatment for panic disorder. *Journal of Consulting and Clinical Psychology, 78*(6), 964–973. https://doi.org/10.1037/a0021067

Thrasher, S., Power, M., Morant, N., Marks, I., & Dalgleish, T. (2010). Social support moderates outcome in a randomized controlled trial of exposure therapy and (or) cognitive restructuring for chronic posttraumatic stress disorder. *Canadian Journal of Psychiatry, 55*(3), 187–190. https://doi.org/10.1177/070674371005500311

Tilli, V., Suominen, K., & Karlsson, H. (2012). Panic disorder in primary care: Comorbid psychiatric disorders and their persistence. *Scandinavian Journal of Primary Health Care, 30*(4), 247–253. https://doi.org/10.3109/02813432.2012.732471

US Census Bureau. (2020). *National population by characteristics:* 2010–2019. https://www.census.gov/data/tables/time-series/demo/popest/2010s-national-detail.html

Van Dis, E. A. M., van Veen, S. C., Hagenaars, M. A., Batelaan, N. M., Bockting, C. L. H., van den Heuvel, R. M., Cuijpers, P., & Engelhard, I. M. (2020). Long-term outcomes of cognitive behavioral therapy for anxiety-related disorders: A systematic review and meta-analysis. *JAMA Psychiatry, 77*(3), 265–273. https://doi.org/10.1001/jamapsychiatry.2019.3986

Ventis, W. L., Higbee, G., & Murdock, S. A. (2001). Using humor in systematic desensitization to reduce fear. *Journal of General Psychology, 128*(2), 241–253. https://doi.org/10.1080/00221300109598911

Vitousek, K., Watson, S., & Wilson, G. T. (1998). Enhancing motivation for change in treatment-resistant eating disorders. *Clinical Psychology Review, 18*(4), 391–420. https://doi.org/10.1016/S0272-7358(98)00012-9

Westra, H. (2004). Managing resistance in cognitive behavioural therapy: The application of motivational interviewing in mixed anxiety and depression. *Cognitive Behaviour Therapy, 33*(4), 161–175. https://doi.org/10.1080/16506070410026426

Whisman, M. A. (1990). *The use of booster maintenance sessions in behavioral marital therapy.* University of Washington.

White, K. S., Payne, L. A., Gorman, J. M., Shear, M. K., Woods, S. W., Saksa, J. R., & Barlow, D. H. (2013). Does maintenance CBT contribute to long-term treatment response of panic disorder with or without agoraphobia? A randomized controlled clinical trial. *Journal of Consulting and Clinical Psychology, 81*(1), 47–57. https://doi.org/10.1037/e525102013-009

Windle, E., Tee, H., Sabitova, A., Jovanovic, N., Priebe, S., & Carr, C. (2020). Association of patient treatment preference with dropout and clinical outcomes in adult psychosocial mental health interventions: A systematic review and meta-analysis. *JAMA Psychiatry, 77*(3), 294–302. https://doi.org/10.1001/jamapsychiatry.2019.3750

Wolf, A. W., & Goldfried, M. R. (2014). Clinical experiences in using cognitive-behavior therapy to treat panic disorder. *Behavior Therapy, 45*(1), 36–46. https://doi.org/10.1016/j.beth.2013.10.002

World Health Organization. (2016). *International statistical classification of diseases and related health problems* (10th ed.).

Yonkers, K. A., Zlotnick, C., Allsworth, J., Warshaw, M., Shea, T., & Keller, M. B. (1998). Is the course of panic disorder the same in women and men? *American Journal of Psychiatry, 155*(5), 596–602. https://doi.org/10.1176/ajp.155.5.596

Zwanzger, P., & Rupprecht, R. (2005). Selective GABAergic treatment for panic? Investigations in experimental panic induction and panic disorder. *Journal of Psychiatry and Neuroscience, 30*(3), 167–175.

8 Appendix: Tools and Resources

The following materials for your book can be downloaded free of charge once you register on the Hogrefe website.

Appendix 1: Agoraphobic Cognitions Questionnaire
Appendix 2: Body Sensations Questionnaire
Appendix 3: Mobility Inventory for Agoraphobia
Appendix 4: Panic Attack Record and Daily Mood Record
Appendix 5: Common Cognitive Distortions in Patients With Panic Disorder
Appendix 6: Questions to Help Challenge a Negative Thought
Appendix 7: Interoceptive Exercises Worksheet (Therapist Version)
Appendix 8: Interoceptive Exercises Worksheet (Patient Version)
Appendix 9: Fear and Avoidance Hierarchy Form
Appendix 10: In Vivo Exposure Practice Worksheet

How to proceed:

DOWNLOAD

1. Go to www.hgf.io/media and create a user account. If you already have one, please log in.

2. Go to **My supplementary materials** in your account dashboard and enter the code below. You will automatically be redirected to the download area, where you can access and download the supplementary materials.

   Code: B-EX754I

To make sure you have permanent direct access to all the materials, we recommend that you download them and save them on your computer.

Appendix 1: Agoraphobic Cognitions Questionnaire

This is a **preview** of the content that is available in the downloadable material of this book. Please see p. 95 for instructions on how to obtain the full-sized, printable PDF.

Name: _____   Date: ____/____/____

Below are some thoughts or ideas that may pass through your mind when you are nervous or frightened. Please indicate how often each thought occurs when you are nervous. Rate from 1–5 using the scale below.

1	2	3	4	5
Thought **never** occurs	Thought **rarely** occurs	Thought occurs **during half of the times**	Thought **usually** occurs	Thought **always** occurs

… when I am nervous.

Please rate all items.

I am going to throw up	1	2	3	4	5
I am going to pass out	1	2	3	4	5
I will have a brain tumor	1	2	3	4	5
I will have a heart attack	1	2	3	4	5
I will choke to death	1	2	3	4	5
I am going to act foolish	1	2	3	4	5
I am going blind	1	2	3	4	5
I will not be able to control myself	1	2	3	4	5
I will hurt someone	1	2	3	4	5
I am going to have a stroke	1	2	3	4	5
I am going crazy	1	2	3	4	5
I am going to scream	1	2	3	4	5
I am going to babble or talk funny	1	2	3	4	5
I am going to be paralyzed by fear	1	2	3	4	5
Other ideas not listed (please describe and rate them):					
	1	2	3	4	5
	1	2	3	4	5
	1	2	3	4	5

Reprinted with permission by Dianne L. Chambless, ©1984. Questionnaire available at https://web.sas.upenn.edu/dchamb/questionnaires/

Appendix 2: Body Sensations Questionnaire

> This is a **preview** of the content that is available in the downloadable material of this book. Please see p. 95 for instructions on how to obtain the full-sized, printable PDF.

Name: _____   Date: ____/____/____

Below is a list of specific body sensations that may occur when you are nervous or in a feared situation. Please mark down how afraid you are of these feelings. Use the following five-point scale.

1	2	3	4	5
Not at all	Somewhat	Moderately	Very	Extremely

... frightened by this sensation.

Please rate all items.

Item	1	2	3	4	5
Heart palpitations	1	2	3	4	5
Pressure or a heavy feeling in chest	1	2	3	4	5
Numbness in arms or legs	1	2	3	4	5
Tingling in the fingertips	1	2	3	4	5
Numbness in another part of your body	1	2	3	4	5
Feeling short of breath	1	2	3	4	5
Dizziness	1	2	3	4	5
Blurred or distorted vision	1	2	3	4	5
Nausea	1	2	3	4	5
Having "butterflies" in your stomach	1	2	3	4	5
Feeling a knot in your stomach	1	2	3	4	5
Having a lump in your throat	1	2	3	4	5
Wobbly or rubber legs	1	2	3	4	5
Sweating	1	2	3	4	5
A dry throat	1	2	3	4	5
Feeling disoriented and confused	1	2	3	4	5
Feeling disconnected from your body; only partly present	1	2	3	4	5
Other ideas not listed (please describe and rate them):					
	1	2	3	4	5
	1	2	3	4	5
	1	2	3	4	5

Reprinted with permission by Dianne L. Chambless, ©1984. Questionnaire available at https://web.sas.upenn.edu/dchamb/questionnaires/

Appendix 3: Mobility Inventory for Agoraphobia

> This is a **preview** of the content that is available in the downloadable material of this book. Please see p. 95 for instructions on how to obtain the full-sized, printable PDF.

Name: _____   Date: ____/____/____

1. Please indicate the degree to which you avoid the following places or situations because of discomfort or anxiety. Rate your amount of avoidance when you are with a trusted companion and when you are alone. Do this by using the following scale:

1	2	3	4	5
Never avoid	Rarely avoid	Avoid about half the time	Avoid most of the time	Always avoid

Circle the number for each situation or place under both conditions: when accompanied and when alone. Leave blank situations that do not apply to you.

Places	When accompanied	When alone
Theaters	1 2 3 4 5	1 2 3 4 5
Supermarkets	1 2 3 4 5	1 2 3 4 5
Shopping malls	1 2 3 4 5	1 2 3 4 5
Classrooms	1 2 3 4 5	1 2 3 4 5
Department stores	1 2 3 4 5	1 2 3 4 5
Restaurants	1 2 3 4 5	1 2 3 4 5
Museums	1 2 3 4 5	1 2 3 4 5
Elevators	1 2 3 4 5	1 2 3 4 5
Auditoriums/stadiums	1 2 3 4 5	1 2 3 4 5
Garages	1 2 3 4 5	1 2 3 4 5
High places	1 2 3 4 5	1 2 3 4 5
Please tell how high:		
Enclosed spaces	1 2 3 4 5	1 2 3 4 5

Open Spaces	When accompanied	When alone
Outside (for example: fields, wide streets, court yards)	1 2 3 4 5	1 2 3 4 5
Inside (for example: large rooms, lobbies)	1 2 3 4 5	1 2 3 4 5

Riding in	When accompanied	When alone
Buses	1 2 3 4 5	1 2 3 4 5
Trains	1 2 3 4 5	1 2 3 4 5
Subways	1 2 3 4 5	1 2 3 4 5
Airplanes	1 2 3 4 5	1 2 3 4 5
Boats	1 2 3 4 5	1 2 3 4 5

Driving or riding in car	When accompanied					When alone				
At any time	1	2	3	4	5	1	2	3	4	5
On expressways	1	2	3	4	5	1	2	3	4	5

Situations	When accompanied					When alone				
Standing in lines	1	2	3	4	5	1	2	3	4	5
Crossing bridges	1	2	3	4	5	1	2	3	4	5
Parties or social gatherings	1	2	3	4	5	1	2	3	4	5
Walking on the street	1	2	3	4	5	1	2	3	4	5
Staying home alone	1	2	3	4	5	1	2	3	4	5
Being far away from home	1	2	3	4	5	1	2	3	4	5
Other (specify):	1	2	3	4	5	1	2	3	4	5
	1	2	3	4	5	1	2	3	4	5
	1	2	3	4	5	1	2	3	4	5

2. After completing the first step, circle the 5 items with which you are most concerned. Of the items listed, these are the five situations or places where avoidance/anxiety most affects your life in a negative way.

Panic Attacks

3. We define a panic attack as:
   1. A high level of anxiety accompanied by...
   2. strong body reactions (heart palpitations, sweating, muscle tremors, dizziness, nausea) with...
   3. the temporary loss of the ability to plan, think, or reason and...
   4. the intense desire to escape or flee the situation (Note: This is different from high anxiety or fear alone).

Please indicate the number of panic attacks you have had in the past 7 days: _____

How severe or intense have the panic attacks been?

1	2	3	4	5
Very mild	Mild	Moderately severe	Very severe	Extremely severe

4. Many people are able to travel alone freely in the area (usually around their home) called their safety zone. Do you have such a zone? If yes, please describe:

   a. its location:
   _____
   _____

   b. its size (e.g., radius from home)
   _____
   _____

Reprinted with permission by Dianne L. Chambless, ©1984. Questionnaire available at https://web.sas.upenn.edu/dchamb/questionnaires/

This is a **preview** of the content that is available in the downloadable material of this book. Please see p. 95 for instructions on how to obtain the full-sized, printable PDF.

Appendix 4: Panic Attack Record and Daily Mood Record

This is a **preview** of the content that is available in the downloadable material of this book. Please see p. 95 for instructions on how to obtain the full-sized, printable PDF.

Please complete both of the following monitoring forms every day. These forms are important for three reasons: (1) to understand more about your anxiety, (2) to help customize the treatment to you, and (3) to measure your improvement treatment progresses.

Instructions for Panic Attack Record

Please carry several copies of the Panic Attack Record with you at all times and complete one as soon as possible after you experience a panic attack. Note the date, the time it began, and the duration of the attack (excluding any anticipatory anxiety or anxious feelings after the attack). Place a check mark on the sheet to indicate if you were alone or with someone at the time and circle to yes or no to indicate whether or not the panic attack occurred during a stressful situation. For example, if you find going shopping, driving, or going to a party stressful, then this should be rated as such. Circle to yes or no to indicate whether you expected the panic attack or whether it took you by surprise, and rate the maximum anxiety/fear that you experienced during the peak of the attack. Finally, **underline** the first symptom that you experienced, and then check all of the symptoms that you experienced during the panic attack.

Instructions for Daily Mood Record

Please complete this form once per day, preferably at the end of the day. After the date put a rating (using the 0–8 scale provided) for the *average* or background level of anxiety – that is, how anxious you felt in general. Next, put a rating for the *highest* point that your anxiety reached at any time that day (e.g., if you went to a job interview or thought you had lost your wallet). The next two ratings refer to your *average* or general feelings of depression and pleasantness overall that day. Next, please list all medications you took that day, including the dose (in milligrams). Finally, please put a rating to indicate overall how much you *worried that you may experience a panic attack* that day. We realize that this feeling will vary from situation to situation, but we would simply like an indication of your *overall fear of having a panic attack* that day.

Make certain that you keep all the forms together and bring them to your session each week.

Panic Attack Record

Name: _____

Date: _____/_____/_____   Time panic attack began: _____   Duration (min): _____

With: Friend _____   Stranger _____   Family _____   Alone _____

Stressful situation?   Yes   No

Expected?   Yes   No

Maximum anxiety during attack

0	1	2	3	4	5	6	7	8
None	Mild		Moderate			Strong		Extreme

Underline the first symptom you experienced and check (✓) all symptoms that were present:

Difficulty breathing   _____

Racing/pounding heart   _____

Choking sensations   _____

Sweating   _____

Trembling/shaking   _____

Nausea/abdominal upset   _____

Chest pain/discomfort   _____

Hot/cold flashes   _____

Numbness/tingling   _____

Feelings of unreality   _____

Unsteadiness/dizziness/faintness   _____

Fear of dying   _____

Fear of losing control/going crazy   _____

This is a **preview** of the content that is available in the downloadable material of this book. Please see p. 95 for instructions on how to obtain the full-sized, printable PDF.

Daily Mood Record

Name: _____   Week ending: _____

Each evening before you go to bed please rate your *average* level of anxiety (taking all things into consideration) throughout the day, the *maximum* level of anxiety you experienced that day, your *average* level of depression throughout the day, and your *average* feeling of pleasantness throughout the day. Next, please list the *dosages* and *amounts* of any medication you took. Finally, please rate how worried or frightened you were, on average, about the possibility of having a panic attack throughout the day. *Use the scale below to help you.*

Level of anxiety/depression/fear of panic attack:

0	1	2	3	4	5	6	7	8
None	Slight		Moderate			A lot		As much as you can imagine

Date	Average anxiety	Maximum anxiety	Average depression	Average pleasantness	Medication type, dose, number (mg)	Average anticipation / worry about panic

This is a **preview** of the content that is available in the downloadable material of this book. Please see p. xx for instructions on how to obtain the full-sized, printable PDF.

Appendix 5: Common Cognitive Distortions in Patients With Panic Disorder

This is a **preview** of the content that is available in the downloadable material of this book. Please see p. 95 for instructions on how to obtain the full-sized, printable PDF.

Common Cognitive Distortions in Patients With Panic Disorder

Cognitive distortions represent inaccuracies that commonly occur in our patterns of thinking. Cognitive distortions become problematic when people become anxious or panic, because they can exacerbate the symptoms of anxiety and panic, which in turn can make the thoughts seem more valid. As a result, people often engage in maladaptive behaviors (i.e., avoidance) to cope, which unfortunately prevents the development of adaptive coping skills and eliminates the opportunity to assess the accuracy of the thoughts. Therefore, learning to identify distortions in your thoughts is an important step in breaking the vicious cycle of panic.

There are many lists of common cognitive distortions that are widely available on the internet. Though the names and definitions may differ slightly, they all serve the same purpose: to help people catch potential errors in their thoughts and break negative patterns of thinking.

The two *most common* cognitive distortions in people with panic attacks and anxiety disorders are:

Catastrophic misinterpretations: This involves assuming the worst possible physical outcome. For example, people with panic may catastrophically misinterpret an otherwise benign bodily sensation (e.g., increased heart rate) that occurs spontaneously or for good reason (e.g., exercise) as a sign of impending doom (e.g., heart attack).

Probability overestimations: This involves the belief that a *possible* (though unlikely) outcome is *certain*. For example, they may believe that if they are dizzy or faint then they are certain to pass out or if they have a panic attack they will "lose control" or "go crazy" and end up on a psychiatric inpatient unit.

Two *additional* cognitive distortions that commonly occur in people with panic attacks and anxiety disorders are:

Underestimations of ability to cope: This involves the belief that if faced with a challenging situation, the person would not be able to cope with it. For example, the person may believe that if they experienced a panic attack while far from home, they would become confused and lost and not be able to find their way back home. Or if they experienced a panic attack at work or school, they would not be able to function and would have to quit/withdraw.

Emotional reasoning: This involves the belief that our emotions are always an entirely reliable gauge of reality. For example, when people with panic feel anxious, they often assume that there must be a valid reason for their anxiety and look around for evidence to support this belief. If they link it to a particular agoraphobic situation, they often try to "escape" from it or avoid it to keep themselves safe. If they cannot find a threatening external situation, they then often turn their attention inward, scan their body for any elevated sensations (which are likely to be found, since they are anxious to begin with), and then conclude something bad must be happening to them.

Appendix 6: Questions to Help Challenge a Negative Thought

> This is a **preview** of the content that is available in the downloadable material of this book. Please see p. 95 for instructions on how to obtain the full-sized, printable PDF.

Questions to Help Challenge a Negative Thought

When you feel anxious, in addition to searching for any cognitive distortions in your thoughts (see handout on Common Cognitive Distortions in Patients with Panic Disorder) it can also be helpful to evaluate them for their accuracy (and, if accurate, their helpfulness), by using any (or all) of the following questions below. As is the case for a list of the most common cognitive distortions, additional lists of questions to help challenge negative thoughts are widely available on the internet.

- What is the evidence that this thought is true?
- What is the evidence that this thought is not true?
- Am I confusing a possibility with certainty? It may be possible, but is it probable?
- How many times has what I am fearing happened before?
- Am I 100% sure that what I am fearing will happen this time?
- Are there any other possibilities? How likely are they?
- Am I confusing a thought or emotion with a fact?
- Is my thinking being influenced by the way I am feeling?
- Will my thoughts change if my feelings change?
- What would I tell a friend if they had the same thought?
- What would a friend say to me about my thought?
- What is the worst that could happen?
- What is the best that could happen?
- What is most likely to happen?
- If the worst-case scenario happened, what could I do to cope with it?
- If the worst-case scenario happened, would it be a horror or more of a hassle?
- If my thought is true, is there some productive action I can take now to help the situation?
- If my thought is true, and there is nothing I can do, how is it helpful to keep thinking this way?

Appendix 7: Interoceptive Exercises Worksheet (Therapist Version)

> This is a **preview** of the content that is available in the downloadable material of this book. Please see p. 95 for instructions on how to obtain the full-sized, printable PDF.

Interoceptive exercise conducted	How long it was performed	Predicted SUDS (0–10)	List of all sensations experienced	Intensity (0–10) of sensations	Similarity (0–10) of sensations to a "real" panic attack	Maximum SUDS (0–10)	List of all anxious thoughts experienced

Appendix 8: Interoceptive Exercises Worksheet (Patient Version)

> This is a **preview** of the content that is available in the downloadable material of this book. Please see p. 95 for instructions on how to obtain the full-sized, printable PDF.

Please use this worksheet to track practice of interoceptive exposure. Completing this worksheet will allow you to understand more about your feared bodily sensations and to measure your improvement treatment progresses. At a minimum, you should practice at least 4 times per day (twice at the start of the day and twice at the end of the day). When completing the exercises, it is critical that you experience the sensations as fully and intensely as possible, for as long as possible, while making every attempt to not avoid experiencing the sensations by ending the exercise early or the use of safety behaviors. Complete the first three columns before doing the exercise. Complete the remaining columns immediately after finishing each exercise.

Interoceptive exercise practiced	Date/time practiced	Predicted SUDS (0–10)	How long it was performed	List of all sensations experienced	Intensity (0–10) of sensations	Similarity (0–10) of sensations to a "real" panic attack	Maximum SUDS (0–10)	List of all anxious thoughts experienced

Appendix 9: Fear and Avoidance Hierarchy Form

> This is a **preview** of the content that is available in the downloadable material of this book. Please see p. 95 for instructions on how to obtain the full-sized, printable PDF.

Situation	Fear	Avoidance

Appendix 10: In Vivo Exposure Practice Worksheet

> This is a **preview** of the content that is available in the downloadable material of this book. Please see p. 95 for instructions on how to obtain the full-sized, printable PDF.

Please use this worksheet to track practice of in vivo exposure. Completing this worksheet after each practice will allow you to understand more about your feared situations and to measure your improvement treatment progresses. At a minimum, you should complete at least one in vivo exposure exercise per day. At first, it may be best to follow the items in the order they were placed on the fear and avoidance hierarchy you created. However, as you progress in treatment you may also want to mix up the hierarchy items and even incorporate new and naturalistically occurring (i.e., unplanned) situations into your practice routine. Toward the end of treatment, you should be focusing on the items that you predict will cause you the *most* distress and looking for any new situations that make you anxious. Complete the top half before starting each exercise and the bottom half immediately after finishing each exercise.

Date: _____/_____/_____

In vivo exposure item to be practiced: _____

Pre-exposure SUDS (Anticipatory Anxiety): _____/10   Predicted Max SUDS: _____/10

Feared outcome (be specific!): _____
_____
_____

Strength of belief in feared outcome before (0–100%): _____%

How long was exposure task performed: _____ minutes

Post-exposure SUDS: _____/10   Actual Max SUDS (at any point during exposure): _____/10

Results of feared outcome (be specific!): _____
_____
_____

Strength of belief in feared outcome after (0–100%): _____%

What was learned about feared outcome (be specific!): _____
_____

Strength of belief in what was learned about feared outcome (0–100%): _____%

Comments about this practice, including anything that surprised you, any difficulties that were encountered, any safety behaviors used, and what adjustments could be made next time:
_____
_____
_____
_____

Peer Commentaries

Dr. Simon Rego, one of the leading figures in the world in the practice of evidence-based cognitive behavioral treatments, has now produced a superb treatise on the nature and treatment of panic disorder and agoraphobia (PDA). This very readable and compact description contains every bit of information clinicians would need to know about PDA to administer these interventions, including diagnosis, assessment, and the theory and process of treatment itself, all presented in a concise, easy to understand format. A case vignette of a very typical, albeit severe, case provides an additional helpful illustration. Every clinician will want this little book on their bookshelf.

David H. Barlow, PhD, ABPP, Professor of Psychology and Psychiatry Emeritus, Founder, Center for Anxiety and Related Disorders at Boston University, MA

I am quite impressed by the comprehensive and accessible approach offered in Dr. Rego's book Panic Disorder and Agoraphobia *outlining the full range of evidence-based procedures for this condition. His clinical expertise shines through in the clear explanations of cognitive behavioral therapy strategies provided, making it an invaluable resource for professionals and even individuals seeking to manage their symptoms on their own. I found the section on therapists' fear of using the various exposure strategies particularly relevant as this can often lead to less effective treatment, especially for those therapists new to utilizing this treatment. The book concludes with a case example that brings the case conceptualization and treatment strategies to life. Overall, I highly recommend this book for clinicians interested in state-of-the-art evidence-based treatment for this common, debilitating condition.*

William C. Sanderson, PhD, Professor of Psychology, Director, PhD Program in Clinical Psychology, Director, Anxiety & Depression Clinic, Hofstra University, NY

Panic Disorder and Agoraphobia *by Dr. Simon A. Rego is a concise, practical, and complete hands-on guide to understanding and effectively treating this challenging clinical problem. The practicing clinician will find everything that they need to evaluate, diagnose, and treat patients. Written in clear prose, this will be a useful reference and guide for all clinicians.*

Robert L. Leahy, PhD, Clinical Professor of Psychology in Psychiatry, Weill-Cornell Medical College, New York, NY

This exceptionally accessible guide offers a comprehensive overview of panic disorder and agoraphobia, paired with proven strategies for effectively treating this challenging condition. It is an invaluable resource for clinicians new to treating these issues, for those seeking to deepen their expertise, and for supervisors and trainers guiding others in delivering cognitive and behavioral therapies for anxiety and related disorders. I recommend it wholeheartedly!

Martin M. Antony, PhD, ABPP, Professor of Psychology, Toronto Metropolitan University; Author of the *Shyness and Social Anxiety Workbook* and *The Anti-Anxiety Program*

This book stands out as an exceptional resource for clinicians and students seeking a comprehensive, evidence-based approach to understanding and treating panic disorder and agoraphobia. What makes it unique is its concise yet detailed structure, practical focus, and user-friendly tools like clinical pearls and checklists that directly enhance practice. Targeted towards mental health professionals and trainees, this volume serves as both an invaluable day-to-day guide and a continuing education resource for those aiming to refine their expertise in treating anxiety disorders.

Jonathan S. Abramowitz, PhD, Professor and Director of Clinical Training, University of North Carolina at Chapel Hill, NC

How to treat trauma survivors effectively

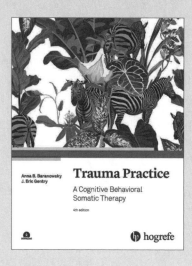

4th ed. 2023, xii + 228 pp.
including online material
US $59.00 / € 50.95
ISBN 978-0-88937-592-5
Also available as eBook

Anna B. Baranowsky / J. Eric Gentry

Trauma Practice
A Cognitive Behavioral Somatic Therapy

This popular, practical resource for clinicians caring for trauma survivors has been fully updated and expanded. It remains a key toolkit of cognitive behavioral somatic therapy (CBST) techniques for clinicians who want to enhance their skills in treating trauma. Baranowsky and Gentry help practitioners find the right tools to guide trauma survivors toward growth and healing. Reinforcing this powerful intervention is the addition of a deeper emphasis on the preparatory phase for therapists, including the therapists' own ability to self-regulate their autonomic system during client encounters.

Over 40 video and audio demonstrations of many of the techniques are available for download. There are also 36 handouts for clients that can be downloaded and printed for clinical use.

"Carefully researched, theoretically grounded, and beautifully written, *Trauma Practice* is a must-read for any clinician who treats interpersonal trauma."

Robert T. Muller, PhD, Professor, Faculty of Health, York University, Toronto, ON, Canada

www.hogrefe.com